Collected Poems

PATRICIA BEER

Collected Poems

CARCANET

First published in 1988
Published in paperback in 1990, 1997
by Carcanet Press Limited
4th Floor, Conavon Court
12–16 Blackfriars Street
Manchester M3 5BQ

A CIP catalogue record for this book
is available from the British Library

ISBN 0 85635 863 0

The publisher acknowledges the financial assistance
of the Arts Council of England

Printed and bound in Great Britain by SRP Ltd, Exeter

To the Same

(for Damien)

'My favourite poem in this anthology
Is William Cowper's *To the Same*' I wrote
At school. The English mistress pointed out
That this was no true title, but to me
Even after half a century
It shines out with the steadfastness of gold
From a dark bookcase. It is a title held
By all achievers in fidelity.

I do not write love poems, but if I did
I too would praise the continuity
Of love and not the onset. So a name
Would not be necessary, for I should
Of course mean you, who have survived with me,
And address all my sonnets to the same.

Contents

7

The Lie of the Land (1983)

Introduction

A few years ago I read an article about Hans Christian Andersen which concentrated on his life rather than on his work and set out a list of his principal anxieties. I was struck by this list because though most of them are probably experienced by most people, three of them if taken allegorically sound like ones to which poets are particularly prone: a fear that one's house will burn down, a fear of being bitten by mad dogs, and, above all, a fear of being buried alive.

As an intelligent person he took steps to deal with these three terrors. When he travelled he packed a rope in his luggage and always had one ready at home. When he saw a dog coming down the road, however well-balanced it seemed at a distance he crouched in somebody's doorway until it had gone by. And when he felt like sleeping he put a notice by his bed saying 'I am not really dead.' It was his most eloquent bedtime story.

A *Collected Poems* is a way of saying 'I am not really dead.' (*Complete Poems* suggests that one might well be and *Last Poems* that one demonstrably is.) It was recently brought home to me that I needed such a statement. I live a pleasant family life in the country, winning few prizes, wielding no power, exercising no patronage, reviewing only from time to time and appearing on television only every so often, with the result that last spring, when an interesting piece of work was being allocated, somebody authoritatively told somebody else that I was dead. This was irritating but not untreatable. I began to compile a *Collected*.

Another experience I hope this book will protect me from is that of being judged only by the very early poems. Not long ago I was giving a reading in a north-country town to a group of cruel old women who had elected to savage 'The Fifth Sense', a poem I wrote in 1957 and had not included in my programme. One of them went so far as to say that the epigraph – an extract from a provincial newspaper – was the only good thing about it. The daffodil-haired tutor, who obviously believed that rude was astute, nodded encouragingly as each banderilla was planted.

After a while I exerted myself to ask if they would mind attacking some other poem of mine as this one had been written a quarter of a century earlier and had been succeeded in the course of time by over two hundred others which I would be much readier to defend. It turned out that it was the only one they had ever read; the tutor had photocopied it out of some balding anthology for the occasion. I know that neither he nor his class will buy or borrow *Collected Poems* but I feel that the existence of the volume may help to avert such situations.

The earliest of these poems were written in the mid-Fifties and the latest just before the book went to press. I have included only a few from *Loss of the Magyar* which was published in 1959. At the time, this volume, though generously received in some quarters, also brought the killer bees out in force, led (if killer bees have leaders) by Roy Fuller in the *London Magazine*. Killer bees are not noted for flexibility of behaviour and I have no wish to repeat the experience.

My introduction to modern poetry was bizarre. The fact that I had not met any before I went to university was quite natural. Teachers in East Devon in the Thirties, even if they had come across the work of Eliot and Pound, which I imagine they had not, would have disliked it, and they could hardly have been expected to know the work of Auden, Spender, MacNeice and Day Lewis who had only recently started publishing. At university modern poetry was being regarded by the staff with general suspicion and light laughs, and of course was not on the syllabus. What I read for myself was exhilarating, but without guidance or encouragement it was only spasmodically so, and I had my degree to think of. I once saw Day Lewis plain, being shepherded to a reading by the committee of an avant-garde poetry group, but that was the nearest I got.

After university I went to Italy and there I stayed for seven years, devoting myself to its language, its inhabitants and its literature. I met Montale briefly. I talked about Montale a great deal. I fashionably looked down my nose at Quasimodo. I came back to England in 1953. Dylan Thomas had just died and a greater number of women than was quite practicable were claiming past intimacy with him.

I had written no poetry since my schooldays. I had written a great deal then and had never ceased to think of myself as a poet, though so far manquée in adult life. Now, back with my native language – which had become rather objective, a language one taught to other people – I wished to start again.

It was a bad time to do so. There I was, thoroughly informed about English poetry up to the end of the nineteenth century but almost totally ignorant of what had been done in the twentieth. The poetic scene I stepped into was inevitably a death-trap. It was really the scene of the Forties still. The Movement had begun to stir but was not yet under way. *The Hawk in the Rain* had not yet been published. The myth-kitty had not yet been sneered out of existence; to many it was still Aladdin's cave.

I had come back, in fact, to a land where such verses as these were what poets and poetry lovers were admiring and aiming at:

> We wove in the mantle of the king
> Grapes grey as human breath at dawn.
> In the nave, four ladies sleeping
> The dead one on their breasts have borne.

*   *   *

> You were adventure's web,
> the flag of fear I flew
> riding black stallions
> through the rocky streets.

*   *   *

> I wish you anguish and wild seas
> Cataclysms and thunder
> So that in extremity you long for me
> And the bed of my gender.

The mode was so pervasive that the poems translated at that time – from the French, the Greek, the Spanish, the Czech – not only sounded exactly like each other but exactly like those being written in English.

Poetry like this came in for a rare trouncing in the later Fifties. One critic called it, rather prematurely, the nadir of twentieth-century verse. Another described it as verbal debauchery. Yet another said it was lush and loose. But at the time of my return to England I was greatly taken with it. My mind was a vacuum as far as the writing of poetry was concerned. I had realised by now that I had to cast out the techniques of former centuries but had forgotten what the Bible says about the devils that come surging into empty rooms. Unconscious that I was indulging in debauchery of any kind or standing at the nadir of anything, I wrote as lushly and as loosely as I could.

Of course I do not blame the poetry of the Forties. I do not really blame myself either, for what I did felt more like a sensible adaptation to the climate in which I had landed than deliberate and systematic imitation. In fact I have never been accused of imitating any particular poet. Craig Raine, it is true, writing not so long ago in the *London Magazine* said that my work reminded him of that of E.J. Thribb, but I took him to mean that there was a natural resemblance, not that either of us had imitated the other. But I was certainly affected by the poetry of the Thirties and it shows all too clearly in *Loss of the Magyar*.

I soon went on from there, to extensive reading of much better poetry and to an attempt at hard thought about what I was trying to do. History has been given so many rude names, such as bunk, that to say the rest is history, though it is hardly original and suggests exhaustion of the theme, does not indicate conceit. The point is that once a *Collected* is out the reader has all the evidence from which to form a fair opinion, for better or worse, and does not need comment from the author.

Nevertheless there are a few remarks that someone who has been publishing poetry regularly for thirty years may be allowed to make, simply to put herself in place. And I now turn to the first person plural. I do not mean that we poets are a happy few – a miserable many is more like it most of the time – and we are certainly not a band of brothers; as Ted Hughes said about the creatures of the sea: 'In that darkness camaraderie does not hold.' But we have co-existed for three decades and been subjected to the same temptations and blights. Only a collection can show what any of us eventually made of them.

Growing up as a poet appears to need one of the skills that is essential to growing up as a human being: the ability to recognise and resist bullying. The poets of my generation have met with a great deal of it. A. Alvarez has tried to bully us into being less genteel; for our own good, of course. Our audiences at poetry readings have demanded that we go confessional, that we go popular, that we go American, with threats that if we do not we shall be labelled, as the case may be, cold, academic or parochial. Since the Forties, various translators have put pressure on us to share, even emulate, the feelings of East Europeans who have had a wider and harsher political experience than ourselves.

I have always enjoyed Marianne Moore's comment: 'Poetry is an imaginary garden, with real toads in it.' Few poets, I guess, would question its accuracy. The toads serve many useful purposes. For one thing they present a challenge, and the result is that the garden also contains many real volumes of *Collected Poems*.

Patricia Beer

Early Poems
from *Loss of the Magyar* (1959)
and *The Survivors* (1963)

The Fifth Sense

A 65-year-old Cypriot Greek shepherd, Nicolis Loizou, was wounded by security forces early today. He was challenged twice; when he failed to answer, troops opened fire. A subsequent hospital examination showed that the man was deaf. NEWS ITEM, December 30th, 1957.

Lamps burn all the night
Here, where people must be watched and seen,
And I, a shepherd, Nicolis Loizou,
Wish for the dark, for I have been
Sure-footed in the dark, but now my sight
Stumbles among these beds, scattered white boulders,
As I lean towards my far slumbering house
With the night lying upon my shoulders.

My sight was always good,
Better than others. I could taste wine and bread
And name the field they spattered when the harvest
Broke. I could coil in the red
Scent of the fox out of a maze of wood
And grass. I could touch mist, I could touch breath.
But of my sharp senses I had only four.
The fifth one pinned me to my death.

The soldiers must have called
The word they needed: Halt. Not hearing it,
I was their failure, relaxed against the winter
Sky, the flag of their defeat.
With their five senses they could not have told
That I lacked one, and so they had to shoot.
They would fire at a rainbow if it had
A colour less than they were taught.

Christ said that when one sheep
Was lost, the rest meant nothing any more.
Here in this hospital where others' breathing
Swings like a lantern in the polished floor
And squeezes those who cannot sleep,
I see how precious each thing is, how dear,
For I may never touch, smell, taste or see
Again, because I could not hear.

Sabine Farm

Say he was small, grey-haired and loved
Hot sunshine. When the blaze of Rome
Licked up July and August, he was here
Motionless while the goats moved
Under the ilex. This was home,
The sun no more than he could bear.

The wine he grew was sweet; it bloomed
Scarlet among the stones, was drunk
Noiseless as heat. The afternoon stream
Quietly as the clouds foamed.
Under elephant leaves it sank
Into a mute into a jungle dream.

Mosaic on the bedroom floor
Had shapes like handkerchiefs, no boys,
No dolphins. Here he lay in the hills,
Thought of his health, his character,
His art and all the country joys
He knew, flimsy as nightingales.

If he remembered how he fought
At Philippi, the old defeat
Was steamed out like a crease
Here. And the morals he taught,
Sage in the field and yard, were light
As the shadows of the shining geese.

And in this slanting countryside
No road was nearer than the one
Which clicked under horses in the dark
Far down the valley, when the tide
Of market, leaving the little town,
Drew back the farmers to their work.

The Wake

In his tall room my grandfather lay dead.
Downstairs late afternoon lurched like a bee
Round the perennial hearth shadowed with mourners
And the coals shone and clicked like gorse in bloom.

We two found grass and snow in his room.
Green veins flickered in the marble chimney
And the river-green eyes of the little girl, my sister,
Flashed with swans as she looked up.

He was higher than we and quiet as a cliff
That still upholds the weight of men and horses
Though so near to crumbling that the first slither of dust
Must already have picked unfelt at the air.

He was the Alps against the setting lamp
And in his heights we heard no news at all.
Only a bell nodded its way round the mountain
As the warm everyday beasts went home.

Death of a Nun

Here lies Mother Agnes, nun
Who died last night, eighty years old.
Standing beside her, all I see
Is that her flesh has turned to gold.
Not even the tawny parlour blinds
Could make my skin as rich as hers.
Her roots of dying must have sucked
The yellowness of clay and stars.

In former days the holy man
Went up the mountain we are told,
Drew back out of the scorching light
And could not see his God for gold.
It seems as though this nun has stepped
Into the lightning of her death
And captured what she always had,
Contained it, brought it down to earth.

There is no kindness in her face
Nor love, but then there never was.
Love is a symbol, does not need
To see its features in the glass.
Her charity was pure. It lay,
Is lying still, along the bone,
No firmer now her heart is stiff
And metal stands in every vein.

Her name was buried when she took
Her vows, as if her life of prayer
Was uttered from the nerves and cells
Of one who was not really there.
No more impersonal now dead,
No more anonymous and cold,
She is transformed to precious stuff
That bears a general name, like gold.

It should not come as a surprise
To see the beads that she has clutched
Lying across a hand as hard
As any limb that Midas touched.
The alchemy of her disease
Has worked a long-maturing spell
And turned her into gold, yet made
No change in anything at all.

Roman Road

After a hundred cypress trees the road
Swerves out of its straightness just as if, to end
    A hundred placid days,
      Some seventh wave broke there.

Perhaps there was once a tomb, some deeply-felt
Monument, the road had to avoid.
    A stone stood in the air
      Above the grave in those days

When accoutrements and flesh, recently visible,
Had not quite foundered into bone and rust.
    Though there is nothing there
      Now, the track still swerves

And, weighted by a memory too deep
For crumbling, it seems suddenly to plunge
    Pulling the horizon in
      Like a draw-string purse.

So many years have passed since the road builder
Shrugged out of his course to please the dead
    That daylight travellers
      Accept it, notice nothing,

But in the dark, returning into Rome,
They feel the familiar route shy like a horse
    Stumbling on old blood
      To bring them home alive.

They know then that the dead must not be left
To sleep alone, they must be tampered with,
    For a forgotten grave
      Will make the highway curve.

Wordsworth

Winter was not a symbol, nor was spring,
Nor was the corpse that floated to the air
After a week of water, nor the wing
Of the December star pinned to the mere

By a child's skate. His dawns were literal,
His ghosts did not melt with the ice of darkness
But froze on into the sunshine. Guilt was real
And the stern mountain had no other likeness.

A lake was something that could drown him, though
It danced, he said. The river had no voice
Although it sang. He knew too well the plan

By which the world shared neither grief nor joy
And stood for nothing else, but really was
The wet and dry, the hot and cold of man.

Vampire

'When I was whirling on the wind,'
He said, 'I saw a light.
I would have passed a darkened house
But in the flowing night
This lantern had a heart of sponge
That sucked me from the tomb.
It was the shining of her need
That lit me to her room.

She could have hung up garlic flowers
And shut the window tight
And rocked a child of flesh and blood
Under a shaded light.
Her beauty was resistible
For all her shining head
It was the shining of her wish
That lit me to her bed.

Down in each safe harbour
The moth-brown ships are pinned,
So why must she put out to sea
In all this wrecking wind?
Why must she play the castaway
Sprawled in an open boat?
It was the shining of the waves
That lit me to her throat.

Her sisters gather in the room
And loudly take her part.
Her brothers seek a pointed stake
To hammer through my heart.
She suffers, as she meant to do,
And as she knew she would.
It was the shining of her pain
That lit me to her blood.'

Port Royal, Jamaica

'In this place dwelt Horatio Nelson. You who tread his footprints,
remember his glory.'

The sea, heavy with jellyfish, jointed
With sharks, is completely present here.
It would be impossible to go anywhere
Except by water, or be nudged to glory.

Land persists, reefs under the skin of sea
Ready like tomorrow's pox. White flagstones
Where he walked do not heave or roll
But their steadiness is temporary, not the norm.

Under the guango trees he thought in terms
Of oak, wood on water with a hollow heart
Where men instead of sap moved and pushed.
Ashore he had three mistresses who died.

Their crosses are nearby, hopeful like anchors.
Up the road there is a church full of boys
Who, innocent, experienced yellow fever,
Swelled like sheep who have eaten clover.

Morgan's drinking vessel is there also,
Purged now and used for Holy Communion.
Henry Morgan, pray for us. Sea disinfects
Even the pirate's gibbet and so does glory.

Sea is danger, but is a path out of death
Too. It is easy to remember Nelson
And tread his footprints, for whatever we do
Because we do not wish to die, is glory.

Witch

I shall see justice done.
I shall protect time
From monkish, cowardly men
Who say this life is not all
And do not respect the clock.

On those who will not escape
I shall see justice done.
I have courage to use
Wax and the killing pin
On behalf of prisoners.

I cut off the pilot's thumb
Because his compass failed.
I shall see justice done
Whenever the homeward bound
Mistake their true home.

In my black pointed heart
I cherish the good of all.
With storms, potions and blood
I shall see justice done
For I know goodness well.

Never shall bogus love –
Habit, duty or weakness –
Win any mercy from me.
By the light of my long burning
I shall see justice done.

The Flood

Noah, looking out of the safe Ark,
Saw, glum as any geographer,
Waterlogged the map of the world sink.
All dry hedges, every crisp park
Were being lowered to their burial, far
Down under the rains, to grow rank.

The sea crept on and upwards with a chill
Giggle over the stomachs of whatever
Could not float. And at length Noah saw
Standing on top of what was the last hill –
A single stepping-stone now with no shore –
The last survivors who had run all the way

Out of their homes and families to be saved:
By height alone for Noah could not stop.
The sea rising stretched them out tall enough
Tiptoe on a rack where they no longer moved,
Taut every neck and every instep
In catapult longing to be up and off.

But this was not the last which Noah saw
Of them. They did not sink with the land. Learners
From desperation, hope happened to them.
Though there was no inch of world left, though
There was no help in sight, or near, or corners
To conceal it, they began to swim.

This was an ignorant way to meet fate,
Hoping. There was not much intelligence
In the eyes now riding level in the water.
Spitting out death and not swallowing it
Was merely postponement, it showed want of sense.
Sooner would have been more sage than later.

But less admirable. There has been some doubt
Among Noah's descendants about hope.
Perhaps because they come from those in the Ark
And not the swimmers, they give hope great weight,
Thinking it not illusion, the final jape,
But the last firework strong and shrewd in the dark.

Epitaph in a Country Churchyard

We all came here out of the long grassy fields
One day when the saint's flag cracked on the church tower
Or when the dark rain flicked on the porch like ink.
We were all brought here inert, but I chose.

We all moved only because they carried us
But a compass twitched in my hand. My father,
My grandfather came here, even those choked at sea
Swallowed a token of earth here, but I tasted.

There was nothing personal about our bringing low.
The country-wide Black Death and the local warlock
Did not select us. But I picked on myself
To come through the smell of nettles to the smooth spade.

I was no suicide, for so doing I would
Have forfeited the final luck of the lost daughter.
I agreed to lie here, understanding who I was.
We all perished, but I died in my own sleep.

Beatrice-Joanna

Heroine of *The Changeling*

Fear no more the lack of the sun.
Darkness was not what you wanted
But day will never come again
Because you took the light for granted.
Dawn of which you never dreamed
Will break for you in being damned.

Fear no more the eyes of the just.
You have cheated to the goal,
Thrown an apple down for lust
And then run far beyond them all.
Hurry to your bridegroom's bed
With your borrowed maidenhead.

Fear no more the hand of the good.
You have broken off his finger.
Bury it, that so his blood
May not scratch you any longer.
Grace and beauty will not leave you
But there is no one to forgive you.

Fear no more the kiss of the rogue
Nor the murder on his breath.
You must have him like the plague,
Sicken through him to your death,
Cough him off your lips and go.
Stone dead has no bedfellow.

Finis

Now he is being shot. The last page
Is a mere nail-tip away; he will surely die.
The first bullet jerks him into old age,

The second shows him a sight secretly.
But I, the reader, feel no surprise
Though he walks in spurts over the dry

Carpet to bed, for I recognise
What he is doing. It is his last food
He must gulp now, so down he lies

Pulling the bullets and the blood
In with him, curling up around them,
Hugging them tight to do him good.

Into each organ, into each limb
He pulls back strength. With his coiled breath
He lassoes what has run from him.

Drawn up like a tortoise on a path
He retracts everything. This is the end.
Yet it looks more like life than death.

'The Girl I Left Behind Me'

To all those who have left
Someone else or themselves
Behind, the marching song
Is dedicated like a book
That in some way applies.

The person left behind
Could nag with chaste prayers,
Or might have turned whore,
Or might be a careless ghost,
But could not disappear.

The soldiers vowed return
And perhaps some did,
Hanging up their red coats
Inside a bedroom door,
Kissing with outdoor breath.

How were they received?
Was there pique in the finger-nails
Running over their backs
At having had to wait
For the war to turn round?

Were they received at all?
Perhaps anything left
Behind cannot be found
Again, neither the girl
Nor the one who marched off.

Out of Season

My mother who died young
In an outlandish rhythm
Would have been seventy now
And perhaps dead in funeral time.
So I may start to mourn
As I would celebrate
The first or second birthday
Of a still-born baby.

Any premature death
Can be borne, can be lamented
When the clock strikes
The latest hour there is:
The breath of the potholer
And the miner's tap
Must have stopped by now.
No one could last so long.

It could not happen before.
A mile as the crow flies
Means nothing, either to crows
Or humans; it could not happen.
Pegasus took to the air, chosen,
But did not really arrive
Till the first wingless horse
Had kicked back the last league.

Just Like the Resurrection (1967)

The Postilion has been Struck by Lightning

He was the best postilion
I ever had. That summer in Europe
Came and went
In striding thunder-rain.
His tasselled shoulders bore up
More bad days than he could count
Till he entered his last storm in the mountains.

You to whom a postilion
Means only a cocked hat in a museum
Or a light
Anecdote, pity this one
Burnt at milord's expense far from home
Having seen every sight
But never anyone struck by lightning.

Overseas Student

This year they have set us
Lady into Fox.
I know what a lady is,
Smell, timbre and sex,
But not the other word,
It does not exist here.
So far I have not dared
To open the book. Fear
Of what the lady faces
Is better in ignorance.
If she goes into tight-laces
Or falls into a trance,
It would be quite harmless,
But in this huge hot land
Where so much is formless
I feel I cannot stand
Reading of some machine
That sucks her in perhaps,
Some angel she becomes, some queen.
Possibly two strong lips
Will take her, but will she then
Be in the stomach or the heart
Of a heroic man?
Shall I ever be able to start?

Lemmings

Lemmings die every year. Over the cliff
They pour, hot blood into cold sea,
So that you half imagine steam
Will rise. They do not part company
At first, but spread out, a brown team
Like seaweed, undulant and tough.

Light changes, and the wind may veer
As they swim out and on. The sea
May become sleek or shrewish. Foam
May blind them or may let them see
The wet horizon. It takes time.
They do not die within an hour.

One by one they leave the air
And drown as individuals.
From minute to minute they blink out
Like aeroplanes or stars or gulls
Whose vanishing is never caught.
All in time will disappear.

And though their vitality
Does not look morbid enough
People call it suicide
Which it has some appearance of.
But it may well be that the mood
In which each year these lemmings die

Is nothing worse than restlessness,
The need to change and nothing else.
They have learnt this piece of strand
So thoroughly it now seems false.
They jump, thinking there is land
Beyond them, as indeed there is.

On the Cobb at Lyme Regis

Here no one wins because no one contends.
The white wall curves, wheels, skating out to France,
And I walk on it, between warm water
And cold, little boats and leviathans.

Dangerous the sea is; for all I know
It is even now, underneath the skin,
Battering the sea-wall with drowned sailors
Or countrymen who carelessly fell in.

But there is no Poseidon any more
To rise with a seventh wave and thunder,
To turn on all taps and overwhelm me
Gone suddenly shapeless like a spider.

If I had magic to keep the sea down
I would feel exceedingly complacent
And walk the wall like Nelson at Port-Royal
Conscious of skill to blunt any trident.

But this safety is different. I know
From my teachers what is impossible.
I am in no danger, the sea cannot rise,
Which is the most frightening thing of all.

Scratch-path

Usually a scratch is a flaw
That would make a rosewood desk cheap
Or spoil a forehead for three days.

But computers depend on them.
Only through a scratch-path can they
Remember, and go the same way

Again. And even spongy brains
Live principally on scratches,
That make wood and skin suffer so.

Four Years After

'The perfectly preserved body of a British mountaineer was found near Courmayeur yesterday more than four years after he fell to his death on the Géant glacier.'

Yes, this was my husband, I
Cannot say 'is' though he has
Not changed since his dying day
Four years ago. Certainly
Ice is strong as saintliness
To keep corruption away.

I have altered in these years,
Better or less rightly wed,
Uglier or handsomer
Than I was then. All my tears
Rolled, grief like cargo shifted,
Grew and was cut like my hair.

I have moved but he not once,
For fifty moons not one cell.
Look at his glassy aplomb
Which has not been splintered since
Out of death and life he fell
To nothing. I could kill him.

Brunhild

My father laid me in a ring
Of fire, and then like thunder rolled
Away, though I had been more close
To him than in his arms. He told
Me I should never see his face
Now he had voiced me like a song,

Made me a separate thing, no more
His warrior daughter but a woman.
But I do see his face, I see
It all the time. Though I am human
He can still rule. He promised me
That a brave man should break the fire,

A man he would approve of, no
Tentative weakling. He will have
My father's dominant beard and mighty
Shoulders, and instead of love ＿
This obligation to be doughty.
I wait for the entrance of the hero

Dressed up in my father's fashion.
If I were free to love I would
Decide on someone thin and shaven.
But in the ring I lie like wood
Or soil, that cannot yield or even
Be raped except with his permission.

Gallery Shepherds

Shepherds on old hills, with robber
And wolf lurking
Think themselves not so much seers
As hard-working.

But in paintings the mother of a god
Often blesses
Those who tend wool bodies topped
By wasp faces

And indeed shepherds are mostly shown
Simple and wise
In pictures, finding out things
Before spies.

Primed they come in from the country
To a small town
Thinking it glorious Gomorrah
That will burn.

Angels have spoken of a marvel
For countrymen
Who are portrayed as if gaping
At a con man.

The town needs them; they are followed
By knowing rich
Kings, entirely urban, whom the artist
Paints as such.

The Clock

The oldest clock we have
Stops every few days.
The weights catch on the case
And do not go right down.

It has the appearance
Of any eight-day clock.
We respect its size, not
Winding it like a watch.

The relative who gave
It to us used to say
A stopped clock foretells death,
Not thinking us so rash.

We have refuted this
Already, but it is
So easy to hear death
In the silence of stairs

Where once a pendulum
Thudded like a cart-horse
That now a deep meadow
Has swallowed, you can see

How some poets, like Donne,
Have 'used themselves in jest
By feigned deaths to die',
A run-through for the dark,

A drill. Obviously
Death cannot come each time
The clock stops. It may be
Good practice to think so.

Lion Hunts

A lion is never a lion in a royal hunt,
Only a victory to cheer the king up.
Sometimes six men carry him upside down,
His tail stiff as a leg, though his dewlap
Must be soft still because they grasp it.
He started proudly and knew when to stop.

Sometimes he stands, shoulder high to the king,
Nearly as good as the king, almost man to man.
Only his bare genitals and the ten weapons
Growing out of his paws show he is not one.
More honour to the king who is about to kill him.
A little of the blade has already gone in.

Years later he is in colour, so is the king
And they fight among pink rocks. A prince lies
Restfully dead, a cub watches to learn.
Magenta blood spurts from the lion's thighs
And the king's, but the curved sword is itching.
It must always be the animal who dies.

Pardoner's Tale Blues

I am Death, all bone and hair
    Mother, let me in
Get no health from this country air
    Mother, let me in.

What shall I do till Death can die?
What shall I do till he lies down
Till he lies down with his eyes at rest?
What shall I do till he dies?

Yes, God made me to live forever
    Mother, let me in
No deep earth and no deep river
    Mother, let me in.

Well run along men, to your bag of gold
    Mother, let me in
I cannot laugh, I am too old
    Mother, let me in.

And I knock upon the ground with my staff
    Mother, let me in
I can joke though I cannot laugh
    Mother, let me in.

Leaping into the Gulf

Children do not ask the proper questions
Of themselves, or so they come to think
Long afterwards. I do not feel I should
Have wondered who Curtius was, and why
He leaped and with what consequences.
Laziness and knowing that a painting
Was not a history lesson, absolved me then,
Forgive me now. But why did I not say:

A man who holds his shield up against nothing
Is mad, surely? A man who drops the reins
As though a horse needs no guidance through air
Has no sense of responsibility.
A horse that puts its head down, its behind up,
Like a dog trying to look harmless,
Can it be desperate? Should the hero wear
The artist's face without his spectacles?

A glare on paint was all I really saw,
Something inside a frame to goggle at,
A work of art. I certainly never laughed
At Haydon, as I hear so many did.
I simply stood there, well-grown for my age,
Bandaged and blindfolded and gagged,
Near a gulf, too, but very far from leaping.
I would as soon have answered my mother back.

The Return of the Prodigal

The point of no return
Would have been easier to fix
Perhaps than the moment

When I decided to leave the house
Where the lovers cried like peacocks
If they were not too drunk,

Where men urinated all over the place,
Where the pigs ate disgusting messes
And the dog almost nothing.

Certainly there was a point in time
When I put one bandaged leg forward,
Jolting the sores, and bent

The other leg with the bare knee,
Ready to walk to the gate, to shift
The cow lying across it

And start on the journey home.
I did so. I remember doing so.
But the decision took place

Either yesterday or this morning
As I was thinking it all over
Some fifty years later.

Poets' Corner

Here I come, the poet Drayton,
Quite convinced of my salvation

Through the death of Christ the Son,
In the year sixteen thirty-one,

But not convinced of fitting honour.
In heaven there is no poets' corner,

Only sinners saved by grace.
I may not get a special place.

I put my earthly laurel down
And reach out for a heavenly crown.

O God, who art creative too,
Recognize me, give me my due,

And now my worldly leaves have faded
Let me not remain bareheaded.

Head of a Snowdrop

After the north-east wind I carried
A snowdrop indoors. Taut as a bead
And bright, it lay in a bottle-top,
Nothing but petal from the wound up.

Its roots, stem, were still out of doors; strange
That away from them it could so change,
Normally opening into flower,
Wide as a primrose in one warm hour.

Human fingernails and hair move less
After death and lack naturalness.
Births after death – young Macduff – have such
Horror they can be used by a witch.

Anti-vivisectionists show men
Keeping dogs' heads alive, yapping even.
Schoolboys studying the Stuarts laugh
About Charles talking with his head off.

And I have this freak on my own hearth
Making me think about roots and birth
By false analogies and ignore
Its fulfilled purpose: an open flower.

Concert at Long Melford Church

Long Melford church is built of flint and glass,
The tombstones make your teeth ache
And the paths leading up to it look
Particularly hard through so much soft grass.

Today a concert in afternoon light
Gives the church a more brittle purpose
Than usual, more capable of close.
From this people will go home free tonight.

And there are so many. A Suffolk Festival
Has brought everybody out from London
Like a saint or a marvel. The proportion
Of living men to graves is medieval.

We were taught not to walk on graves as children.
Holding flowers for grandparents, we worked out
Where each corpse would be, walked round it,
Steering past the heels, elbow and chin

Of those submerged and dangerous bodies.
But today the paths and the narrow porch
Cannot contain those coming out of church
During the interval, into the sun and yew trees.

They spread all over the churchyard. They scan
The crowd, recognize, smile and shake hands.
By each tombstone a well-dressed person stands.
It looks just like the Resurrection.

Christmas Carols

They say a maiden conceived
Without so much as a kiss
At the time or afterwards.
Gloria in excelsis.

They name the eternal hall
Where we arrive to wine, fire,
Together and loving, but
Dead. *Quam dulcis est amor.*

Although in their description
Every midnight is clear
So that angels can be seen
Without peering, *hilariter,*

We know better in our fear
And avoid most carefully
David's city after dark.
Honor tibi, Domine.

In a Country Museum

This is a strange museum. In one square yard see
A mummified ibis and a postilion's boot.
Grey litter fills the house. For years every dead man
Had some cast-off curious object to donate.

Mindless and slovenly it is, but in one room,
Close to five jars that once held Daffy's Elixir,
Lies something that takes shape. A pallid patchwork quilt
Wrapped in cellophane, is spread on a four-poster.

A card describes the maker, a fourteen-year-old
Servant girl, with no book-learning and no siblings,
Who saved up half-a-crown for the big central piece
Of cloth, and got up at dawn on summer mornings.

This sounds sober and worthy, but the card goes on
To say that, interviewed at eighty, Mrs Brew
Declared it had given her much greater pleasure
Than anything in all her life. If it is true

That to labour on these plodding squares meant more
Than marriage bed, children and a belief in God,
It is the best country marvel in this building
And suitably placed among these bright fields of food.

Summer Song for me and my Aunts

Never forget the moors
Behind the house, never
Let being a woman
Or the baking of bread
Or sizing up a sermon

Keep you off the heath
And far from the stone wall
That is no more than gauze
To these strong winds.
Headaches come indoors.

Walk uphill from the house
And the graves already there.
The chill of waterfalls
Cannot cause worse coughing
Than sprig-papered walls

Where you die in turn
On a narrow sofa
Boxed up from the storm.
Dying women can walk
On the moors without harm.

The Chemist's Dream

When I started on my life's work
My early ambition was bold
To the point of naïveté.
It was to change things into gold,

To make meadows stiffer than corn
Twanging in the wind like a lyre,
To find rabbits in the last swath
Paralysed with gold not terror,

To make towns like missals painted
By lavish monks, a stiff-necked swan,
A gay witch melting in the fire,
Spinning tops brighter than Saturn.

Subtler I next looked for long life,
The elixir of never-die.
The tetchiness of old people
And their hairbreadth sleep bothered me.

I wanted to keep them clever,
To be relied on. I included
Myself in this discovery
But once again was evaded.

For I am poor and past my prime
And now the third part of my quest
Needles me, to find the liquid
That teachers call the alkahest.

It will dissolve everything
It comes in contact with, the noose,
The throne, lutes and battering rams,
It is power, easy to use.

It will create no such problems
As wealth and eternal life set,
Except one, what to keep it in.
Which I will solve when I find it.

Spell

When after many deeds the witch
Buried some bones in my back yard
To bring about my destruction
I could think at last, 'This is hard.'

She had cut a cock's throat at me
Already, but still I grew rich,
Healthy and important, because
I had guilt enough to match

And far more guilt than her first move
Had called for, wax image and pins.
That had been child's play, her evil
Less animated than my sins.

But this burying of bones is more
Than I deserve, two eyes awake
Against two sleeping, so near home,
Such strong gods against guilt so weak.

I speculate from fear: did she
Need a lantern? were the bones wrapped
In anything to be brought here?
Did worms grow restless where she stepped?

My innocence will be the death
Of me. I have lived too chastely
To shore up guilt against these bones.
I have not been killed honestly.

Young Widow

It is a luxury at my age
To say 'I am too old' when asked to marry.
Autumn leaves, fading coals and sunset
Are metaphors to state that I am weary

But no more than that; sunset does not
Become darkness, nor a live coal a dead one.
Perhaps I should have called in the stars
And proved that no one born under Scorpion

Can take up with a Crab. Class or race
Might have been good excuses, or heart scared
By sorrow. It is deft and polite to tell lies
To a suitor. The truth is, I am dead tired.

On Saturday evening I said no,
But on Sunday morning walked in bad weather,
My own mistress, around the churchyard
Where people older than I lay together.

The Baptism

Beloved daughter, you must be
Totally immersed. To douse
The fiend is not the purpose
But because it was once done
By a baptizer called John.
(No Saint, it would be popery,

We are all saints.) If the saints
Stare at your wet frock, let them.
Lust is locked up in a hymn.
I shall stare too. The body
Is a grand chain, even I
Invite my daughter to dance.

It is life to us, this mock death.
Out in the streets the dryness,
The no-water holds menace.
What dance-hall, what cinema
Could provide us with such drama
As taking a virgin's breath?

Afterwards we shall all read
Passages from the Bible
About breasts and the able
Bridegroom who does not dally,
Words which long since turned chilly
And static in my own bed.

I know you have never felt
What I and the brethren have.
This warm-water tank, this grave
Is quite tasteless to the sons
And daughters of Puritans.
They lose everything but guilt.

I have been white hot, have been
Out in blizzards of desire.
If you wake up to stale air
Thank God for this legacy:
I give you with love today
A sixth sense, the sense of sin.

Abbey Tomb

I told them not to ring the bells
The night the Vikings came
Out of the sea and passed us by.
The fog was thick as cream
And in the abbey we stood still
As if our breath might blare
Or pulses rattle if we once
Stopped staring at the door.

Through the walls and through the fog
We heard them passing by.
The deafer monks thanked God too soon
And later only I
Could catch the sound of prowling men
Still present in the hills
So everybody else agreed
To ring the abbey bells.

And even while the final clang
Still snored upon the air,
And while the ringers joked their way
Down round the spiral stair,
Before the spit of fervent prayer
Had dried into the stone
The raiders came back through the fog
And killed us one by one.

Father Abbot at the altar
Lay back with his knees
Doubled under him, caught napping
In the act of praise.
Brother John lay unresponsive
In the warming room.
The spiders came out for the heat
And then the rats for him.

Under the level of the sheep
Who graze here all the time
We lie now, under tourists' feet
Who in good weather come.
I told them not to ring the bells
But centuries of rain
And blustering have made their tombs
Look just as right as mine.

Foam: Cut to any Size

The shopkeeper of whom I know nothing
Except this notice and the hard threatening goods
Drawn up inside his tight window
Probably has no whimsy in him,
Certainly lives ten miles inland.

Whimsical myself, I would say
That to cut foam is not beyond the power
Of someone who keeps files, hammers,
Mangles and mowers, that can change the shape
Of wet clothes, grass and iron.

Of course I know what he means
But the words rattle my ancestors
Who all their lives fought against foam
Which finally jumped down their throats
And cut them, before the crabs could.

Postcard

Snow fell on London Zoo. The Polar bears
Turned grey in half an hour. Quickly they stopped
Looking at the North, for it came flying past.
They saw the cold for the first time in years,
Choosing and nosing one piece as it dropped,
One flake to them smelling of all the rest.

There are advantages in any prison.
Bears have more food here, more security,
Freedom to breed though not much wish to do so.
But now the air is visible and the season
Can be touched, now that they feel and see
Their white stone ledge upholstered into snow,

They sicken for the perils of their home.
We are all lucky perhaps to live away
From danger, to receive only a few
Random cold flakes of fear out of the storm
Massing somewhere else. Yet on a day
Like this, the only safety seems to be

In the great blizzard playing at the pole,
Where danger could become our native land,
The central place, inside this fringe of fear.
And every touch of snow seems to recall
Some light and menacing postcard from a friend,
'Having a lovely time. Wish you were here.'

A Dream of Hanging

He rang me up
In a dream,
My brother did.
He had been hanged
That morning,
Innocent,
And I had slept
Through the striking
Of the clock
While it had taken place,
Eight,
Just about time enough
For it to happen.
He spoke to me
On the telephone
That afternoon
To reassure me,
My dear brother
Who had killed nobody,
And I asked him,
Long distance,
What it had felt like
To be hanged.
'Oh, don't worry, lovey,' he said,
'When your time comes.
It tickled rather.'

A Visit to Little Gidding

This is a place of departure
Not of arrival. Even the signpost
Saying Little Gidding, a shock
To any poetry-lover, seems
Meant to be read retrospectively
By tourists on their way back.

As we rise from the fens to where
The hills begin, the flatlands
Give the impression of leaving
Us rather than being left
And they carry the sun away on them,
Warmth going not cold coming.

The pilgrims have gone; they have been
Here this afternoon with flowers
For Ferrar's tomb, so large a wreath
They were either rich or numerous,
We do not know which, they have gone
And their flowers are bright and dying.

The Scouts camping in the next field
Are lugging tea-urns and dismantling
Trestle tables. It has been visitors'
Day, but the parents have gone
Now, leaving their stalwart sons
Jesting shakily like survivors.

And we must go, if we want to be home
Before dark, for home is not here,
Less here, in fact, than in most places.
We are visiting a famous poet
Who followed a famous king
Who sought out a famous good man

And so on back to the beginning,
Which is the end, where the line vanishes,
Where the mirrors stop reflecting.
And the prayers, the escape-route
And the poem were perhaps
Not light coming but darkness going.

The Best Province

I like it here. Soldiers, administrators
And wives all pull strings to be posted
Here in mid-empire, south of the cold.
I come of rather good family myself.

I like the biggest arenas to applaud in,
To walk beneath trees that are set as puddings
Except at evenings when they boil with pigeons,
To have a choice between sun and shadow.

I like these aqueducts that carry men
And chariots as well as water through the sky
Then let them run free through forests. These Gauls,
Some of them, are nice enough to be Romans.

I should emphatically not have liked
To fight bright blue men in the rain, to head
Letters 'Verulamium' or 'Uriconium'
And enclose proud explanations of failure.

It is not as if I could have made up for it
Afterwards, done well at Hadrian's wall, for instance,
And been sent here by way of promotion.
Some diseases bring permanent loss of balance.

Fellow citizens, get what you want the first time
Round. It is interesting to make a false start,
You could write a book about it or ten poems
But would be happier if you did not have to.

The Estuary (1971)

The Estuary

A light elegant wall waves down
The riverside, for tidiness
Or decoration – this water
Needs little keeping in – but turns
The corner to face the ocean
And thickens to a bastion.

No one can really taste or smell
Where the salt starts but at one point
The first building looks out to sea
And the two sides of the river
Are forced apart by cold light
And wind and different grasses.

I see this now, but at one time
I had to believe that the two
Sides were almost identical.
I was a child who dared not seem
Gloomy. Traversing grey water
From the east side where I was born

And had spent a normal cross life,
To live gratefully with strangers
On the west side, I grinned and clowned.
I did not go back for ages
And became known for cheerfulness
In a house where all was not well.

Grief was a poltergeist that would
Not materialize but broke
Everything. Neither believed in
Nor dreaded, it took one decade
To appear, one to be recognized,
Then cleared the air wonderfully

So that nowadays I am able
To see the estuary as two
Distinct pieces of countryside,
Not a great deal to choose between
Them perhaps but at least different,
Rising normally from two roots.

On one bank, stiff fields of corn grow
To the hilltop, are draped over
It surrealistically.
On the other, little white boats
Sag sideways twice every day
As the sea pulls away their prop.

Looking Back

When Troilus died he was given food
And a hilltop like one more god

High enough up to hear music
Of a new kind. He could look back

On his fighting and on the plain
Where his blood still held the dust down.

Being detached now seemed a skill
He had mastered, not a windfall.

It was very easy at first
From that height to look down on lust,

Note with the cool eyes of a saint
His girl sleeping in Diomede's tent

And dwell on the futility
Of human relationships, free

As a convict in the first five
Minutes before the dogs sniff

After his escape. It was not
Long though before he saw earth start

To turn again and the saddening
Green stain of the spring widening.

Christmas Eve

The roofs over the shops
Are grey and quiet already.
In two hours from now
Light and noise will drain
From counter to cash desk
Into the streets and away.

People will go home
To windows that all year
Turned into their rooms
But goggle outwards now
With lit-up trees.

Tinsel wriggles in the heating.
Everything hangs.

As it gets dark a drunk
Comes tacking up the road
In a white macintosh
Charming as a yacht.

Dilemma

Read about the Buddhist monk.
When seven brigands move through the still trees
To murder him he yells so loud
That businessmen in Peking
Look up, twenty miles away.
We must admire him.

But what a comfort
To see the Queen in corny historical plays
Pin up her hair, thank her ladies,
Forgive everybody and go
With only a sidelong glance
At the man with the axe.

Which ought I to be?

One Man One Vote

My railwayman father voted
Only once in his entire life.
Politics was for the children
Of this present world and not for
Those who were marching to Zion.

He would not even vote Tory
Though he knew they had the breeding
And wealth that could help you, and though
The local candidate's daughter
Had by chance the same name as me.

Yet at sixty-three he went out
One evening, furtive after dark
But swashbuckling, down to the polls
To vote for a man who once worked
On the railways: a guard, Father thought.

The Branch Line

One train was the last.
Decorated with a crowd
Of people who like last things,
Not normally travellers,
Mostly children and their fathers,
It left to a theatrical blast
As the guard for once played
At his job, with mixed feelings.

Photographers were there,
For the only time perhaps
Since the railway groped
Down into these shires
First of all, and the squires
Fretted about their deer.
There were flags and a few maps,
And cheers as the signal dropped.

The platform is now old
And empty, but still shows
The act of waiting.
Beyond it the meadows
Where once the toy shadows
Of funnel and smoke bowled,
Are pure green, and no echoes
Squeeze into the cutting.

The villages that gave
The stations their names
Were always out of sight,
Behind a hill, up a lane,
Dead, except when a train
Fetched somebody forth alive.
But now no one at all comes
Out of them by this route.

If the particular fast
Bright dragon of childhood
Is null, I feel the same,
Extinct; not obsolete

Nor dead, but lightweight.
The line has left no ghost
Even, but is as void
As my discarded name.

My past has been defaced
Because it ran together
So often with this line.
Trains exist elsewhere
But different, sinister:
Heads, looking out for a last
Good-bye, freeze and weather
To the sky, as at Tyburn.

Happy Ending

God guard you, storybook hero,
At risk under the sail which the wind shouts down.
The heroine on land
Sees the edge of the storm in a headache of seagulls
And is already arranging
Her eyes to look without envy
At happy half-couples
Made to be re-united.

Live through the endless rain.
Stamp on the quayside at last
With stiff boots and soft feet.
Quick, send a nosey bystander to her house
With the news, before resignation
Closes her throat.

Within a year teach her to think
That great happiness is a knack
She has learned or was born with.
Before tomorrow morning make her realize
She is not the survivor
But has a very fair chance
Of dying before you.

A Birthday Card

Best wishes for your birthday
Come with a brig in the top
Fifth of the picture, perching
On sea more tentatively
Than the muscular gulls that
Beat the air at its own game.

It is a fine day, towards
Evening. The scarlet sun rolls
Casually down the sky
Which is matt and featureless.
There is not much likelihood
Of shipwreck at the moment.

Four-fifths of the picture are
A cross-section of the sea
Reaching down farther than light.
Here sits a large mermaid. She
Is heavy, with thick bones, wide
Flesh and a tail that would crush

A drowned man's foot if it lolled
On to it. She is patient,
Too sure of herself to be
Otherwise. She combs her hair
Over her breasts which poke through,
And flexes her tail and waits.

She is charming, yellow hair,
Huge bust, a barmaid under
Water. Her red navel
Is a spot flung off the sun.
She has prepared, with bracelets
And an ornate mirror, worth

Wrecking some woman for. Just
Behind her swim two fish, grouped,
One big, one smaller, a touch
That looks both domestic and
Mythical, Adam and Eve
They seem, Mary and offspring.

This card, archetypal as
It is, could suit nobody.
Mother's boy, bitch's victim,
Henpecked husband might all be
Affronted. Everyone else
Would find it irrelevant.

The Bull

The bull on the poster speaks
Trunkless but not just a head.
Up in London to be sold
His white face that all his sons wear
Is a man's fortune.

He was once a danger.
Even across three meadows
His walk gave him away
Bred stories and giggling fright.
Without any rage he was
Thunder in a field.

Nobody except me seems
To notice him by day
But one night after the rush hour
Someone must have done,

Someone who felt the need
To draw a loop out of his mouth
Saying I AM A BULL.

Arms

I was brought up to believe
In the Everlasting Arms
And took comfort for some years
In the fatherly muscle
And grip, but fell out of them
Gradually and in slow
Motion as God dissolved. Fell
Into nightmares about arms

And specially one picture
Of the world lying flooded
With all the animals drowned,
Visible still in one foot
Of water, frozen, never
To wriggle with the tide or
Rustle to pieces. Stiff-legged
The sheep who could not embrace

And flex as the lions could
Nevertheless lay in their
Ramrod protectiveness
Holding each other like bars.
These limbs were not immortal
And, perishing, they woke me
As in a story I heard:
When my grandfather went down

With his brig in the North Sea
On a calm clear evening
There was no wireless to send
Last love on. He put his arms
Round his son and there he stood,
Protector, up to his knees
In death, and that was the last
That anyone saw of him.

The Eyes of the World

When I was a child only one hope
Enabled me to consider death:
Not heaven but the eyes of the world.
In those days it was chiefly the king
Who attracted widespread attention.
When his 'life moved peacefully
Towards its close' no one went to bed
Till dawn, music stopped, cold crowds screwed up
Their eyes at a tiny bulletin
Stuck on the railings. Some of them went
Home to sew loyal black bands on sleeves.

Something like this I felt might make it
Tolerable: if everyone would stare
At my last breaths and speak about them.
Not being a royal child I had
To shine somehow. I worked hard at it,
Turned poet for a lying-in-state
As though comfort came from cut flowers.
A long time ago this was. But still
When I see men on the moon, stepping
Into new dust with a trail of cheers
And phone calls from earth following them
I think of the world watching

And of the subjects caught in its gaze.
For women it was nearly always
Involuntary. Leda, Mary
Were probably at peace in the hours
Before the god assumed his feathers
And swooped. Their sons with their miracles
Became as much talked of as new stars,
The minute of their making described
Everywhere, but brought them pain and were
Finally fitted into the sky.
Mankind still contemplates these women.

The martyrs Latimer and Ridley,
Who more or less chose, obviously thought
It a consolation to be watched.
Walking in the street for the last time
Past the civilized buildings they had
To leave, conversing for the last time,
One cheered the other with fantasies
Of the candle that they would become
After the flare of burning, a small
Focus but hypnotic till doomsday.
Did this help them ten minutes later?

I do not rely on watchers now,
Guessing that all we can count on from
The eyes of the world is that they spot
The trivialities we prefer
To keep dark. In death I quite expect
The audience shut their eyes before we
Shut ours, tiptoe out of the ward, turn
Off the television as the shots
Are fired. I cannot imagine now
Why I believed they were the answer.

The Underground Garage

In late evening we have come back
To the garage, and are now driving
Up and up the ramp, revving
The concrete underworld away behind us,

Where a few cars in the stale light
Are always questing among the settled
Paralysed ones. Now the bad breath
Of the garage meets the no-breath

Outside. Two months ago Hyde Park
Breathed mildly, wetly and its leaves
Fell in a twist of scents. Winter
Has made everything too dead to smell.

With twenty yards to go before
The night, our lamps' beam confronts
A column of dead leaves advancing
Down the tunnel towards us.

Dead, curled, colourless, stiff,
They march away from their trees, and spread
A sort of thin plausible life
Over the concrete. Dead, thrusting.

The Coming of the Cat

Everyone knows the black cat
Who curled up for centuries
On witches' laps, read aloud
From books of spells, was present
At sin even with back turned,
Who wore strange robes like nightgowns,
Looked cross rather than wicked.

Completely academic
To us now that we have one.
By day we love her from strong
To weak, put down food, stroke, tease,
Admire. She is sealed away
From us in an element
Without speech without fingers.

The breathing of air gives us
No common ground, nor does love
Of sun. She might as well be
Underwater, heaviness
Pumped out of her by the sea,
Or placid in fire, beyond
Our burning and our drowning.

Primitive man, I suppose,
Put her wherever she is
When he stepped from pure shadow
Into a dappled hunter's
World and murdered his siblings
As he once thought them to be.
Indoors became his retreat

Though not full sanctuary.
His women pay off old scores
To this day in some countries
Suckling puppies and kittens.
A gesture merely. The cat
Will always be far-fetched now,
An exotic by daylight.

But at night she has begun
To enter into our dreams.
She comes towards us, smoothly
Along the track of her own
Glare, one foreleg stuck out stiff
As a crutch, an aureole
Of claws around her bright foot.

She comes close and mutilates
Us. Daytime scratches and play
Are now deep wounds. We fear her
Especially when she changes.
Twice I saw her turn into
My mother. For my husband
She frequently becomes me.

Neither of us ever kept
A cat before. Middle-age
Is a tricky time for new
Experiences. We live
In town and keep the windows
Shut. We have been taught to take
Our dreaming like medicine.

Night ticks on. Here in Hampstead
No owls hoot and the church clock
In the 'village' is throttled
Till seven tomorrow morning.
Our kitten sleeps, a four-pound
Weight, round and black in darkness,
Pins down the quilt above us.

The Cat in the Tree

If I had been a tough child
And climber of trees it would
Be obvious why my stomach,
My legs and all my senses
Move with our cat as she steps
On to the bough and it bends.

When the garden first let her go
Slinging her against the trunk
And upwards I felt only
Praise of her black rocketing
But as she halts at bird height
To change course and her paws spy

Out her way along the air
Now I experience it.
I see her weight as the branch dips
But it has become mine too.
I look both up at her and
Down with her. I dread falling.

I stand here taking time off
In a torturer's heyday –
The news this morning was bad –
To go back to a simple
Necessary fear, the leaves
Panicking, the wood yielding.

The Killing of Sparrows

I see nothing of the killing of sparrows.
They are laid out on the kitchen floor,
Presents from the killer,
Or so the cat books say.

I looked long and closely at the first.
In death it was full of surprises:
Its beak huge, the only part of it
That was not already shrinking.
More grey feathers than I realized
A sparrow had. Beadiness gone
A prophetic look about its eyes.
Claws changed from movement to gesture.

Secondhand murder.
I indulge the killer.

I look more casually now.
Bigger as the cat grows, as the year goes on,
The dead birds tick and chime
The cat's life away, mine
And the strength of the town house.

The Faithful Wife

I am away from home
A hundred miles from the blue curtains
I made at Christmas and the table
My grandfather brought back from Sorrento.
I am a career woman at a conference.
I love my husband. I value
Both what I own and what I do.

I left the forsythias half yellow,
The bluebells – lifted from a wood in Suffolk
Last year – still tight, the mint surfacing.
I must sweep the paths when I get back.

And here for the past week you and I
Have been conducting a non-affair
That could not even be called flirtation
That could not be called anything
Except unusually straightforward desire,
Adultery in the heart.
Life is so short.

The programme is ending.
11.30 – Conference disperses.
I watch everybody leaving.
It feels like grief, like the guillotine.

Your turn now; go home
With the 'Good-bye, love'
You use to every personable woman.
Get in your large car which ten years ago
Was full of sand and children's things
On summer evenings.
You are middle-aged now, as I am.
Write your notes up,
Fix the rattling window,
Keep your marriage vows. As I shall.

Group of Islands

Jigsaw of a county.
The green sea has unmade a shire

But narrowly.
Nowhere is the sea-bed
Much more than an arm's length away.
Danger is compressed
Into a few feet of ocean
And the navigator's skill
Must be sharper than his funny stories.

Through mild winters and tart summers
Earth and water keep in close touch.
A dog barks at a shag
That holds its breast as high
As an Egyptian cat.
A gob of foam hops into the boat.

People intermarry.
After a traumatic voyage
You see the same faces.
And the wind at its worst
Pierces everybody and strings them together.

Just beyond the last reef,
Where puffins can be spotted in lucky weather,
Down go the rocks without trace, down,
Too deep now to be called submerged,
Into a darkness where no comparisons are possible
Miles below the fields
That raise flowers like tissue paper
And gorse like lions.

Fish Pond in Lisbon

Level and weightless and still
They lie in water. The hot
Leaves of the waterlilies
Overlap in scales and look
Much more like fish than they do.

The flick of water-boatmen
Out in the air twelve inches
Above them looks like motion
As we know it, but the red
Fish lunge forward out of shade

Like a bright idea and seem
Not an act but the mind laid
Bare. They knock against the skin
Of the fish-pond from inside
With the movement of a blush

And while we lean arguing
Over the picturesque bridge
Our mirrored heads are only
Talking points in the red swirl
That cannot reach conclusion.

In Memory of Constance Markiewicz

The kind of woman that men poets
Hope their own and their friends' daughters
Will not resemble, a rarity.

Stepping from silk into uniform,
From earth to dirt, she lit out and left
The green county where her father ruled

Then left her husband and child also
Like an evangelist with a wilder
Calling or a painter feeling trapped.

Women do not usually do this.
She calls to mind Mrs Jellyby
That pretty monster who looked over

Her children's heads into Africa
Though she would not have died, I suppose,
For the good of Borrioboola.

Constance felt the value of bloodshed
As deeply as Pearse and Connolly.
She bespoke a priest to see her through

The bullets, but did not require him
For eleven years and then bloodlessly,
Having gone far past disappointment.

Yes, she became opinionated
And shrill, but had a longer funeral
Procession than most of us will have.

Picture of Workers Resting

You lie cooling and sleeping, the heat
Just round the corner of the haystack
And the work spread out over the field.

Your two billhooks put tidily down
And each pair of shoes taken off look
Much more like a couple than you do

Though man and wife you lie side by side
Apparently trusting each other.
Rest from work seems no real bond at all.

How very old-fashioned it all is.
The cart now stands in a museum
Of ancient crafts, the clothes have rotted.

A Marxist critic says the painter
Understood perfectly your bowed heads
And degradation. Perhaps he did,

But more profoundly, as creator
Not critic, saw his own flesh and blood
Lying there and did not ask himself

If you would have been quick at learning
To read, given the chance or worthy
Landowners, given a piece of land.

Self-Help

I was brought up on notions of self-help,
Not that it was so called and none of us
Had read or heard of Samuel Smiles; perhaps
Fortunately, as his pioneers,
Artists and inventors were all men.
Women could be useful or obstructive,
Hungry, in tears, or steadfast like the wife
Of Flaxman, but they had to play the game
Of Help the Genius till their dying day.

I looked down on ne'er-do-wells and wastrels,
Did homework all the evening, winter and summer,
Took the Scholarship, School Cert and Higher.
It was the only way to rise above
Being a maid or serving in a shop.
All this went with religion very well,
The Christian message seeming to be that if
You didn't help yourself in worldly matters
Nobody else was at all likely to.

It worked, and now I sit in Hampstead Village
On a Georgian sofa reading Samuel Smiles
In paperback with afterword and foreword.
Makers of stocking-frames and bobbin-net
Machines, discoverers of vaccination,
New techniques in surgery and how
To classify the strata of the earth,
Watch late into the fireless night, get up
To foggy dawns, gag at poor food, and strive.

But not together. Each striver is alone.
If by accident they help each other
Or their paths cross it seems quite out of keeping:
As when Scott, the former copying clerk,
Offers a lift – outside, of course – to Kemp
The shepherd's son who was to build the Scott
Memorial. There is no pattern in it.
The individual is on his own
With his furnace or his telescope.

Self-help is dangerous. In the tall half-light
Of the cathedral Galileo could
Have counted years of peril in the swinging
Lamp. Böttger is buried like a dog
At night. And many of the heroes have
The Luddites to contend with. See them standing
Piebald in torchlight, flames and shouts behind them
As their inventions come to grief. Sometimes
Their daughters have to scuttle into pawnshops.

Here I sit reading, intermittently conscious
Of the people in the alley – Cockney
Accents threatening to a countrywoman
Even after all these years – returning
From the wash-house to their bathless flats
In Peabody-type buildings, and of the problem
Children smashing up someone's milk bottles,
Getting nearer. They live now. Unlike
The resolute contenders of my book.

Unlike my father and grandfather
Who worked so hard and never helped themselves,
And unlike me in another sense who might
Have come straight out of *Self-Help* on my worst days,
Practising lawful self-advancement, preaching
It, enjoying its rewards. And through
The white comfortable mist a wind blows holes,
Lays bare the quagmire reaching for us all.
Whispers how soon we could be shouting 'Help.'

Victorian Trains

I Mr Dombey

The whistle blows. The train moves.
Thank God I am pulling away from the conversation
I had on the platform through the hissing of steam
With that man who dares to wear crape for the death of my son.
But I forget. He is coming with us.
He is always ahead of us stoking the engine.
I depend on him to convey me
With my food and my drink and my wraps and my reading material
To my first holiday since grief mastered me.
He is the one with the view in front of him
The ash in his whiskers, the speed in his hair.

He is richer now. He refused my tip.
Death and money roll round and round
In my head with the wheels.
I know what a skeleton looks like.
I never think of my dead son
In this connection. I think of wealth.
The railway is like a skeleton,
Alive in a prosperous body,
Reaching up to grasp Yorkshire and Lancashire
Kicking Devon and Kent
Squatting on London.
A diagram of growth
A midwinter leaf.

I am a merchant
With fantasies like all merchants.
Gold, carpets, handsome women come to me
Out of the sea, along these tracks.
I am as rich as England,
As solid as a town hall.

II Lady Glyde

The gardener is bringing the elegant luggage
Someone got for me as a bride.
I have never ordered anything for myself.
He approaches along the country platform
To receive the present for his children.
The housekeeper has been buying my ticket.
How I wish you were coming with me
Faithful housekeeper. I am going to my death
Away from my unhappy home.
You are self-righteous and less wealthy than I am.
I could rely on you now as though I were very ill.

This track is no way of escape for me.
My enemy, my husband's friend,
Will meet me at the terminus.
Though I run through the sewers of the city for days
Till at last I see round light at the end
The outlet will be barred by a grid.
I am man-handled.

I look down from the carriage window.
I am the fields and the houses
That the railway pushed aside.
The whistle blows. The train moves.

Safe Lives

This actor with the cow-brown sweater stands
Theatrically still. The Albert Hall
Is half-way through an Evening of Free Greek
Music and Drama. We have had a choir,
An orchestra, songs and a guitar,
And now have come to Aristophanes,
Euripides, the Students' Trial, the Edict
On Censorship. Nobody in the audience
Disagrees. It is all very peaceful.

He speaks, beautifully, and dominates.
Last week we saw him naked in a film.
He is Philoctetes, beseeching those
Who come across him with his running wound
And leave him, to show some humanity.
Pleading does not move them so he threatens:
Open your safe lives to the grief of others.
Disaster strikes down the secure. A strange
Remark. Disaster strikes down anybody.

We have good seats, he seems to look at me.
But I am not secure. I have not gone
Mad yet, neither am I very good
At screaming – I should like to be – but I
Am not secure. And no doubt those who heard
Philoctetes raged dumbly back at him
Throttled with terrors as they stood calmly,
Cheerfully even, by the summer sea.

Ezra Pound Leaves Rome

Morning in the city fills empty
Streets wall to wall. The cars have fled north
With frightened politicians in them.
No citizens with handcarts of home
Follow. Those guns are liberators.

Everyone is indoors. If your bell
Fearfully rings it is the 'traitor'
Who has made no plans for this event
Asking you for boots and a road map
Things he has not needed since boyhood.

Which is the road north in a modern
City? How can he find where it starts?
To leave a city on foot is forced
Especially carrying a knapsack
With bread and tea, and a walking stick.

He has been living for a long time
In a world of his own, but now he
Steps into the landscape, heading north,
Almost studying the position
Of the sun, the length of the shadows.

Autobiography

I sailed through many waters,
Cold following warm because I moved
Though Arctic and equator were steady.

Harbours sank as I discarded them,
Landmarks melted into the sky
When I needed them no longer.

I left behind all weathers.
I passed dolphins, flying-fish and seagulls
That are ships in their own stories.

Driving West (1975)

Middle Age

Middle age at last declares itself
As the time when could-have-been
Is not wishful thinking any more,
Is not, say: I could have been at Oxford
If my parents had been richer
Or if the careers mistress had not thought
Exeter was good enough for me.

It is not misunderstanding either
As when at night in the first year of the war
Bombs could have been thunder
And later on in peace
Thunder could have been bombs.
Sights and sounds are more themselves now.

There have been real alternatives.
They have put on weight and yet faded.

Evening walks go past
Where we could have lived:
The coach-house that the mortgage company
Said had too much charm
And not enough rooms.

Everywhere I look it is the same,
The churchyard or the other side of the bed.
The one who is not lying there
Could have been.

Dedication

His lover dedicated a book to him.
'For John'. Great was the pride he took,
Being half literate,
At featuring in a famous book.
Literary high life had been the bait
To get him on the hook.
Now – 'John *who?*', '*Which* John?' – they mentioned his name.

His lover adored him and was never false,
Took him to parties where he got laughed at,
Did not visit him
In hospital, was away when he came out.
Years passed. The union equalled the book in fame
Till the day of the farewell note signed 'John' in the flat.
His lover grieved to the last but died of something else.

John came back from abroad to the old town,
Made his arrangements, went to the funeral,
Stood in a retired place.
Down the path shuffled the sad six-legged turtle
One huge wreath alone on its carapace
With a card the size of a page, each letter a capital,
Where the world could see a message written: 'From John'.

Swatting Flies

The cripple in her cushioned chair
Holds her walking stick in her one good hand
Ready by the window
Waiting for flies to land.

The window has a healing view.
Woods root in green
And flower in blue.

Her husband does the housework
Now and the housekeeping.
Inside glass she sits uselessly
And not birds but flies sing.

A fly comes in to land
Before her angry eyes.
She pounds with her stick again
And again at his buzz.

It is not easy to swat a thick fly
He can fit into strange corners
And not actually die.

And this fly is especially hard to kill.
He stumbles out of range.
Becalmed he and his foe are both
Far out at sea
Waiting for the wind to change.

Female, extinct

Her ribcage is eked out
With bits of wire.
Her bony gloves
Have no marrow in them.

You can take her home
On a postcard
Separately. She once
Stood up with hundreds

As if to bellow
The Hallelujah Chorus.
Her voice fell
Forward into the mud.

Her sons, little dragons,
All lumbered away.
Her skull was probably
Left out for seasons

In a far pasture
Or on a battlefield
To be gathered up
By wilier beings.

The air of the museum
Snuffles in her nose.
Her passionate jaws
Shout 'Give me time.'

The Letter

I have not seen your writing
For ages, nor have been fretting
To see it. As once, darling.

This letter will certainly be
About some book, written by you or by me.
You turned to other ghosts. So did I.

It stopped raining long ago
But drops caught up in the bough
Fall murderously on me now.

Mating Calls

It is not so much the song
Of the hump-backed whale, reaching
Through a hundred miles of sea
To his love that strikes us. We
Can be heard farther than he.

It is not the albatross
Either, with his strident voice
Promising the most tender
'Always' in tones of thunder.
Our vows may well go under.

Some kind of magpie keeps on
Singing, when his mate has gone,
Not only his notes but hers.
This moves us to pride and tears
That love should make us such bores.

To the South

We have seen nobody the whole afternoon.
Nobody picks the olives nor tends the trees.
Grove after striped grove stays neat by magic.
Where could they spring from in any case,
The husbandmen? This vegetable kingdom
Is vast and has no creatures.
The water is too far down.

Coming south through La Mancha it was the same.
There were sheep, diligently eating nothing,
Each one the centre of a globe of dust.
But no men, though fires from the stubble fields
Stood yellow in the glare and did not walk.
A battleground of sunflowers
Sagged black and dead.

The sun moves now and rolls down towards the olive trees
Ladder-rungs of shadow link the rows.

And now at last the mountains rise up blue,
Two-dimensional only but there is ice in them.
Beyond them the works of man wait
From supercilious arches to candied courtyards
Where children and dolls look right.

And the white doves will sleep
Heavy in the palm trees like fruit.

Spanish Balcony

The trains that have been howling
Out on the plain all night
Have gone quiet or away.
Ordinary noises have come back to the town
And light to the balcony
Where today's batch of morning glories
Have begun to stir.

The moon remains, uselessly, in the smooth sky
White and rumpled like a vaccination mark.

Someone puts a melon into a patch of sun
To ripen for this evening. On the pavement
Stands a basket of pig's trotters
Not divisible by four.

Twenty morning glories have come out by now
More than any day this year.
They ride on the heat.

All the clocks in the town are wrong.
Light lowers and one roof leads to another.
This is the time of day when in the churches
Every Madonna dressed in party clothes
Begins to look less out of place.

Twenty blue morning glories have shut for ever.
They lie beside tomorrow's lot,
The same shape, dead or sleeping,
But there is no doubt which is which.

The golden melon has been taken in.
The moon has more point now.
Somewhere the trains are getting ready to howl.

The Bible

Everyone in prison reads the Bible.
If they never wanted to before
They do now: it is an unwritten law.

To prisoners of war the journalist
Offered to send it and a home-made cake.
With loved ones far away you pray and bake.

The swindler starting on his five-year sentence
Reads a portion as he always has
Done, every single day, so his wife says.

A TV documentary about
A certain prison showed the earnest chaplain
Getting the first offender to explain

What he would like. 'A Bi –' 'Yes?' He could not
Believe his ears. 'A Biro' stammered the con.
'Oh yes, of course. Of course I'll get you one.'

The Fittest

A young man of twenty-one
Going into hospital
For his first operation
Re-decorated his flat,
Re-hung the door, and arranged
A great deal more cupboard space.

A man of seventy-one
Bought an old manor house cheap
Because of dry rot so wide-
Spread and firmly established
That it would take a lifetime
To eradicate they said.

A man of eighty-two
Was more gallant to pretty
Girls than he had ever been.
He drove right across Europe
And to crown it all adopted
Five orphans, almost babies.

Jane Austen at the Window

When she was young and dancing,
Pregnant women sometimes took
The floor, shamelessly bouncing,
Treating it as a good joke.

In her middle age they loomed
Always larger and larger.
She pitied them. They were doomed
To lose looks, health and figure.

Poor sex objects, animals,
Slack and worn out at thirty.
She pitied with failing pulse.
They lived on to be eighty.

In her last illness she sat
At the window in a caul,
Watching them lurch down the street
Heavy with a funeral.

In Memory of Stevie Smith

A good-bye said after a party, after the drive home,
Is often final, to be labelled
Months later as the last word, meaninglessly.
The one who goes inside, clicking
The door after a polite pause, and the one who drives
Off still have something to discuss.

There had been friendship, not close, coming late in the day
With darkness already tropically near.
I remember an outing through the lanes near Hereford
With Easter weather and a fantastic
Story about gold plate in a stately home
That made us laugh till the car swerved.

Mrs Arbuthnot, Phoebe and Rose, must have died
Long ago, and Mrs Courtley
Though she had a few years of conversation left.
Mrs Arbuthnot we know became
A wave, a long and curling wave that broke
Upon a shore she had not expected.

Muriel, dressed up to the nines, with even
Her tiara on, must in the end
Have heard death knock, and opened to her beau
With the black suit come to take her out.
The swimmer whose behaviour was so misinterpreted
At last stopped both waving and drowning.

A heroine is someone who does what you cannot do
For yourself and so is this poet. She discovered
Marvels: a cat that sings, a corpse that comes in
Out of the rain. She struck compassion
In strange places: for ambassadors to hell, for smelly
Unbalanced river gods, for know-all men.

Home

Out of the window
I see the opposite roofs
Fitting well like ours.

This house is as warm
And secure as bathwater.
Yet very often

Through the double glazing
I imagine people crying,
Somewhere out there.

Sometimes I can even
Respond, too. This has only
Started to happen

Since the day I said
'I shall never be much use
Out here. Take me home.'

Appearances

Possibly a shadowy cat perhaps a shadow
Curls up on the dressing table beside the mirror.
Flowers on the dressing table are not for the user.
They are fair but come from no meadow.
The mirror is black, reflects black or is broken.
No clothes lie around for any wearer.
Care has been taken
To split the french window wide open for the gazer

On sky streaked with a first coat of paint,
Earth brilliant with Sahara or North Pole,
Shrubs tricking out its skin like patches.
Four people walk crumpled, faint
In the cold or heat, stooping for the first time
On a walk they ran yesterday. All the while
In the breathless room
The black shape curls up, neither hums nor twitches.

Called Home

'Called Home' the Plymouth Brethren used to say
When someone died. Warm, bright corridors
Led to eternal domesticity
And from outside we heard the sound of tears
Being wiped away by God. Shall we gather
At the river? In the sweet by-and-by?
Yes, I sang then. Beyond the bright blue sky
Dead families would always be together.

Loving an atheist is my hope currently.
Believers cannot help. I must have some
Ally who will keep non-company
With me in a non-life, a fellow tombstone
Stuck senseless in cold grass, squinnying down
At father, uncle, grandfather, called home.

John Milton and my Father

Milton was not my father's favourite poet.
Shakespeare was. And you got marks for that
In the Victorian classroom with the brown
Trusses of the pointed roof and the black fat
Stove with the turtle, and always blowing through it
The smell of clothes muggy with country rain.

Milton came second. You earned marks for that.
My father, a conformist to his death,
Would have believed even at the age of ten
This value judgement to be gospel truth.
But when he spoke of Milton to us, we got
Much more than the right answer from his tone.

Seated on his high Dickensian stool
From puberty to impotence, a clerk,
(The chief clerk in the corner in his glass
Box of authority) he felt that work
And the world were a less smelly school
Where seraphim and angels knew their place.

He tasted hierarchy as Milton did
And was enchanted by it: jewelled stairs
And thrones and powers and principalities.
Each night he knelt but glanced up through his prayers
To the mountain where sat golden almighty God
With nothing over him but empty space.

Noises from the School

Half-past-nine and the town school
Is packed and quiet. From the room in which I write
I cannot see it. I go on working and wait
For some stirring of the pool.

Somewhere it must be harvest time.
Flickering voices half an hour ago,
And a firm piano told the neighbours, 'We plough
The fields and scatter'. An odd claim

Coming from concrete and foul air
Where mortar-mixers arrive and a crane builds.
God apparently goes on living in fields
And all the singers live here.

Eleven o'clock, and the first howl
Of playtime, singular as the opening twitter
Of a dawn chorus, and soon after that the skitter
Over the yard of the first football.

Twelve o'clock. Until half-past-one
Screaming again and a harsh clattering yell:
Some child is imitating – a guinea fowl?
Of course not, a machine gun.

Quarter-to-four. The bell to go home.
Down the alley the children die away. I write
In town silence and think of the habitat
From where my comparisons come.

Driving West

New car. One of the great
Roads of the West Country
That Fielding remembered,
Dying abroad. Early

Winter morning with sun.
They make me feel sane and rich,
An eighteenth-century
Monseigneur in his coach

Who when the sparrows hopped
Down to his warm wheels, sure-
Winged but vulnerable,
Suddenly thought of the poor

And when a smiling dog
Trotted across the road,
Sharp-toothed but crushable,
For once pitied the mad.

Mist in the Otter Valley

This morning in vivid
Sun, as the gulls flew in,
Their bold shadows advanced
And landed on the stone
Some time before they did.

The mist has come uphill
Now, bringing the river
With it. White, hemlock-cold
Rising. I have never
Seen the valley so full.

It is still day. There might
Be some life left. Somewhere
Farmers may be ploughing
In a bubble of clear
Air, a pocket of sight.

And though with their valiant
Shadows stripped off them, though
Hidden from what they kill,
The gulls are there somehow.
Not a beak less brilliant.

The Land Girl at the Boss's Grave

What cheap lettering and poor stone
For the tall domineering person
Who gave me work
Thirty years back.

In ever loving memory of Roderick
(Rory). The flowers have gone black
Yet his wife lives
Past thatched roofs

In the Manor House his father bought
From the real squire who went bankrupt,
(A gentleman
To whom people turn.)

My boss, upstart, knew nothing
Whatever about farming
But reaped his failure
In the grand manner,

Handsome in glamorous green corduroys
Scowling down the harvesting cries.
I was sixteen
And the war was on.

The men I worked with were eloquent
About how he was so incompetent
Starting each tale
'He knew damn well...'

When I was grown up and married
Years later, miles away, I heard
That he sold
Field after field.

They brought him in July heat
Through his shrunken land to this plot
Behind the church
Dank as March,

Past the squire's cottage and the inn
Where still the squire and his son
Whose arms it bears
Drink with their peers.

Beloved Rory in white worms creeps
And the land girl who obeyed him weeps
Like a good slave
For Massa in his grave.

In the Field

The sow moves on mincing feet
Across the field to a tree
Stump, lays her chin on the gold
Grain of wood and explores it
To cure her itch, parody
Of a queen on the scaffold.

The goose stands beside the pool.
Light from the water trickles
Along her stomach as though
She was transparent and full
Of it. Sees us and cackles
Around a tongue thick as dough.

The cat comes out of doors, black,
The opposite of the grass,
Except for shining. The sun
Makes her fur smell metallic.
She darts. In her cut-out eyes
Two of the buttercups run.

After Death

Opening up the house
After three weeks away
I found bird droppings
All over the ground floor,
White and heavy on the windows,
On the worktop,
On the cupboards,
On every wild hope of freedom.

I could not find any bird
At first, and feared
Some science fiction mystery,
To be horribly explained
As soon as whatever
It was felt sure
It had got me alone,
A mile from the village.

At last I discovered him,
Weightless and out of the running,
More null than old wrapping paper
A month after Christmas.
No food inside him of course,
He had died of hunger
And no waste either,
He was quite empty.

His desperate ghost
Flew down my throat and my ears.
There was no air
He had not suffered in.
He lay in one place,
His droppings were everywhere
More vivid, more terrible
Than he had been, ever.

Frost on the Shortest Day

A heavy frost last night,
The longest night of the year,
Makes the land at first light
Look spruced up for death,
Incurably white.

But the earth moving fast
Tips the shadow across
The field. It rolls past
Sheep who hold their ground
And into the hedge at last.

Not far behind, a track
Of frost is following
That the sun cannot lick
Completely green in time,
Before night rolls back.

The Customer at the Ship Inn

This is the tavern that Sir Francis Drake
Always patronized in Exeter,
The menu says. Usually in luck,
And flush, in this Shippe out of water
He got annoyed only when clergymen
Declared that it stood in St Martin's Lane
And not Fysshe Street like everybody else.
He said you tend to get that near cathedrals.

I come here often too, red-veined and sprawling,
Stories quite good but rather repetitious.
The devil does not like this cheerful bawling
Under a low roof, and swings his vicious
Tail another way. All the king's men
Retreat as I can tell them to do when
Valium and alcohol and company
Conjure a brave person out of anxiety.

Reprieve is beautiful, although it can
Not pull down the scaffold. Up the wheel
Of the world the galleons begin
To swing, armed to the heart but dodgeable.
Massive and bright soon now they will appear.
No need for some bedraggled mariner
To sweat in with a warning from the coast
To say the might of Spain is on the seas
No need for anyone to write: 'I must
To Plimouth, and another ship than this.'

The Ungifted

The water diviner
Makes us all look silly.
He lends the forked stick, lets
Us try. He knows that none
Here has the gift really.

Nothing happens. We bend
Down as though the gift might
Start, might run down the stick,
At seven feet even
If it did not at eight.

He says he gets a sort
Of vision of water
But without actually
Seeing anything.
Sight is our gift, later.

The stream he finds would not
Surface naturally
Ever. It dives under
The hill opposite, then
Burrows into the sea.

I stand with my hollow
Family by our bright
Green field, a row of shells.
All we can do is dig
A well and prove him right.

The Water Diviner

You could say I embark on the land.
I move like a boat in the grip of water
That lives confidently, well below the wind.

Peaceful without sharks, with no tides turning,
Underneath tree roots and dead horses
It heaves through hell on a fine morning.

It is too deep to speak. It cannot be heard
Except by me, and I can hear it thinking
In a pun, a non sequitur, or a nonsense word.

I am a man erect in a town of impotents
A merchant banker among the feckless
A poet among civil servants.

This green field offers you a miracle.
You do not watch me, finding a stream
But all the water in the world shoving one mill.

The Healer

He could have charmed the warts off Cromwell.
I have seen the pure, peeled hands
Of those he cured.

Poor Mary Tudor
With Philip/Calais written on her heart
And her false pregnancies
Would have been more difficult.

He does not have to touch.
One day he simply stood like dawn
On top of a hedge up Kentisbeare
And ringworm faded from a herd of cattle.
I saw this happen.

He says he failed only once,
That was with his wife's migraine.

Prochorus Thompson

Notice Prochorus Thompson. He has won
A competition with the smallest bones
In the whole churchyard. And the man-size grave
He shares with none tops all the tombstones.

Three months of life two hundred years ago.
From harvest time to ailing in November
He came to nothing much, even that Christmas
Not much for anybody to remember.

But little Prochorus Thompson bides his time.
He is the right length for sight-seers
Who pay no attention to the corpses
That lived for fifty, sixty speaking years.

Evergreen and rank are the paths between
The yew trees, and lichen creeps like evil
Over men who worked hard and dropped dead,
Women at menopause who saw the devil.

The balance of the churchyard must be righted.
May the full-grown dead seem interesting. May all
Children live longer than Prochorus Thompson.
Strangle the church tower and the passing bell.

The Accident

Dear Husband, Please come to me.
Yesterday I fell on these stern rocks
And lie in hospital. I was wrong to walk
Here alone. Please come, for both our sakes.

As I fell I noticed the seagulls above me.
Legs dangling, wings pumping, they yelled
Out of white breast feathers and spotted beaks.
Then their cliff drew them back. They wheeled

Over the bay of quiet sails and outboard motors,
Over the coarse grass and pink flowers
And went home. I was a subject
Of these rocks. They loved theirs.

I fell in obedience to a law
Like any weak citizen. Sympathy
Was their metaphor, flesh to familiar stone.
Forgive my clumsiness. Please come to me.

The Christmas Tree

Outside the world was full, plural,
Plants and beasts ran and roared.

You could say the tree is standing still
And dead quiet, brought indoors alone.
For an hour the cat waited for it to move.
His murderous face is off guard now.

The cat is a scrounger from the farm.
They do not feed him. He has to hunt.
'That's what they'm for.'

Tonight we work at the tree like dressmakers,
In the breeze of its faint healthy smell.

Light will be rounded up and festooned over it.
That's what it's for.

It shall not be burnt.
At Epiphany we will try re-planting it.
It may go yellow while we still hope
And while the spring goes green.

Perhaps it will look down on the thatch yet.

January to December

The warm cows have gone
From the fields where grass stands up
Dead-alive like steel.

*

Unexpected sun
Probes the house as if someone
Had left the lights on.

*

Novel no longer
Snowdrops melt in the hedge, drain
Away into spring.

*

The heron shining
Works his way up the bright air
Above the river.

*

Earth dries. The sow basks
Flat out with her blue-black young,
Ears over their eyes.

*

The early lambs, still
Fleecy, look bulkier now
Than their shorn mothers.

*

In this valley full
Of bird song, the gap closes
Behind the cuckoo.

*

Fields of barley glimpsed
Through trees shine out like golden
Windows in winter.

*

Though nothing has changed –
The sun is even hotter –
Death is in the air.

*

Long shadows herald
Or dog every walker
In the cut-back lanes.

*

A crop of mist grows
Softly in the valley, lolls
Over the strawstacks.

*

Meadows filmed across
With rain stare up at winter
Hardening in the hills.

Festival

The village holds a summer festival
Red robes go down the grey street in the sun.

Dance in time now you are medieval,
Men hidden in hobby horses, green men in bushes.

Golden corn-dollies make you women fertile,
Blue-eyed bellringers peal you to a wedding.

Children and schoolteacher, stomp round the maypole.
Do not forget how to unwind the ribbons.

The church still stands at the centre of it all.
Vicar, say there will now be a short service.

Four-year-old boy, exclaim 'A circus?', joyful.
It is years later than you all think. Oh, be careful.

Poems (1979)

Return to Canterbury

Together, twenty years older
Back to Canterbury again
The same February day as the first
But greyer, colder.

All the way east, snowmen
Hands stuck in their pockets.
Here the comfortless gloves
Of the serious foemen.

Vergers reverently freeze
With scarves on, underneath
Stained glass stories
Of cold babies on cold knees.

The pillars stutter
Into a fluent sentence of stone
Worn steps approach
The heart of the matter.

The mason's hand round the hammer
Must have been purple.
You take and hold my dead fingers
Declaring summer.

Parson Hawker's Farewell

Let no one wear black at my funeral.
I have not let blackness be the friend
To me it could have been. The black storm
Crawling with demons clambered up the sky
Each day. My eyes shrank. I turned away
And the prince demon tore the roof off my house.

I have passed through purple and grey to white.
I am as white now as the ship's figurehead
The sea spat out on the shore one day.
All its paint licked off, it had a body
Still, better without gaudiness, a face
Hinting at what was behind the colours.

I have been compassionate at the lych-gate.
I have been made hateful by drowned sailors
Brought to me every one, some in good clothes
Others piecemeal out of the murk of rock pools
Where the biting and shaking sea at last left them,
Limbs, dispossessed hearts, all begging for burial.

Those storms. 'A corpse ashore, sir.' The words
Make me cringe even as the gap narrows
Between me and the men I every day sent
To resurrection. All ended with me, and I
Have been alone. Even my loving wife cannot
Ward off the blown leaves that presage storm.

My fellow clerics care mostly about food.
They eat pigs' faces: cannibals, narcissists.
With gluttony they disgust their own angels.
What can I tell them? Some Latin name
With a prim mouth and filth in the tail.
They know enough for that. Pigs' faeces might do.

You see, I have rage still. At lifeboatmen
At coroners I have raged, at those who stole
My books, at the demons who chewed up my fields
Forcing me to buy corn. I shall always
Be angry but perhaps with a white heat
That seraphim will sociably glare back at.

Farewell to the bad roads and the steep hills
And London remote. I shall never walk
On the cliffs alone again. My last cats
Whose language I spoke fluently will outlive me.
Peace and defiance be with you all. What matters
Is not money or being feasted but soul safe.

Birthday Poem from Venice

From this swaying city,
Luck. Red peppers bob in the canal,
Red ribbons on hats.

Holy gold is splashed
Everywhere, as if the first Wise Man
Had torn his moneybags.

Everyone fits in here,
Feels at home. One very hot afternoon
A ghost yawned.

We come across
Two slight acquaintances from NW3
Nuzzling at a Bellini.

Gimmicks as usual.
This year it is illuminated yo-yos,
A square full of fireflies.

Through the centuries
Untold valuable things have fallen
Into the water.

A column lies there idle
And leaves a gap-toothed church. One relic
A saint dived for,

Brought back to the shore
To everyone's amazement, doing breast stroke
With steady halo.

Today is paradisal.
A cat, five minutes created, sits with a pigeon.
Happy birthday.

Three Poems from Teolo

I Monastery

Plane trees ruffle the straight road
That leads to this pink palace,
Courtly among fields of maize.
Day and night it hugs itself,
The wedding world on the shelf.
Windows small as a prison
Turn away from the outside
Hill where gold cypresses reign.

Inside the church – stop, stop, stop –
Twenty ruby red lights stare.
Candles rise up in blue air
Massed like the cypresses. One
By one the uniformed men
Enter through a secret door,
Stay a few moments, then dip
And flicker out, seen no more.

Beyond, there is no guessing
For them, much fancy for us.
Perhaps when we hear a crass
Bell clang, men start chanting there
As though handling a ship, or
Prayer sorts them out like the sea.
Meals vanish, lust is passing
And all die inaudibly.

II   Villa

Five statues on the roof, strong smell of hen.
Mannerly house, shoulders and elbows in.
Urban, it makes the grass urbane.

Ionic order, and a country hand
Shaking a duster over the farmland.
Money was stashed away in the gold ground.

Fortress in town, pavilion in a field.
The barns say 'Cut down' and the columns 'Build'.
No wish of pomp or hunger unfulfilled.

Two lanes of water at the iron gate,
One to arrive by in patrician state,
One to work with next day, to irrigate.

Puffy shots from the meadow in half-light,
Stale gunpowder in a stage fight,
Bring down the creatures, leave the lord upright,

And in a frescoed room he eats his meal
With squashed and dying giants on the wall.
Down from the powerful sky beyond they fell.

How many mansions did his father own.
The purple thundercloud, sleep-walking on,
Will spare the house and devastate the corn.

III   Garden

Guides take us past the house
Only to show how modest
The owners were.
Pride is the garden.

It has two spines
Two skeletons pinned
Criss-cross together
The pin a fountain.

Paths are stagnant
In the sun.
Rivers of statues
Writhe between trees.

Do not try the maze.
Jolly priests
Burrow into it,
Come out undermined.

Hedges do not protect.
The sword of the vista
Comes straight at us,
Sticks out of our backs.

The Black Halo

The halo of Judas is black, blacker than nightfall,
The disciple has started to teach
Leading the way
Pointing out his master to the keen killers
Their helmets sweating in the dark air
Their pikes sticking into the sky like fireworks.

The soldiers are preceded
By gentlemen from the city,
Dignitaries in velvet, a torch guiding them,
Charmed to capture the rebel and restore order,
Charmed to have found a traitor to do the kissing.

Eleven gold haloes circling eleven good faces
Jut into the crowd unsympathetically
Wearing a look-at-me nursery expression.

How shocking is the black halo of the traitor
Which blinked out at the touch of skin,
Brilliant as any till the deadly greeting.
It could not disappear, be the plain air
Round the head of an unimportant man.

Jesus looks as red and smug as an apple
Judas is a fox but would eat anything
They cling to each other
They depend on each other.

All this the bystander can see for himself.
The book has told us the sequel:
His goodness charred, he took leave
And hanged himself from a tree.
See his black halo crouching
Up in the leaves like a black cat.

Jury Duty

'Harrods of Oxford Street'
The defendant says.
A mistake is a lie.

'I don't want to know'
The witness says.
So she does know.

'I swear by Almighty God'
Twelve of us say.
No lightning nowadays.

Four hours' talk at the police station
Has fitted into one page of notes.
What were they doing?

Someone has handled
A ratty old jacket
And a smeared TV set.
Someone else has pretended
For five minutes and ineptly
To be a policeman.

Why does defence counsel challenge me?
Do I look prim about cannabis?
Is it my diamond ring?
Am I old?

I go home every night
To handle, to impersonate.

November Evening

Road-sweeper and gardener have gone home.
Today's leaves have been cleared up
But the moon is brown enough for all of them.

The child sets fire to the house
Hoping to see his fireman father
Clanging up the street in uniform.

Nobody now bothers to please.
Frill after frill has blown off
The avenue of skeletons.

And the leaves have come indoors
Up to the bedroom on the soles of shoes.

Windy Night

Twilight is brown and the ghost wind
makes itself a body out of dead leaves,
flaps the seamy side of winter at us,
takes our breath away.

Over the hedge, straight across our path
comes a broomstick fast as wickedness.
The witch and the cat have been blown off.
It cannot harm us,
only fellow humans throw accurately.

The leaves were slow yesterday and incomprehensible,
now like a chess game speeded up they make sense.

The wind's passion is more convincing
than the law of where it should prevail.

Six months ago beginners, the leaves
are old hands now. They deceive.
Is it a leaf or a field mouse
that scampers out of the grass and dodges back?

The stars look brilliant and useful.
That Plough would work.

No one in these lanes sweeps up leaves
but they will go in time, and perhaps bequeath
the radiance of a Roman floor
where once a mosaic sparkled.

Perhaps the sky will be smooth at dawn
and two or three white tough clouds
Armada across it.

Son

I was not there at my father's death
But happy with a live loved-one
In a hot country. People must scorn me
And the cemetery is sharp, with autumn nagging.
For I did not pick the coffin or the hymns
Or choose the flowers that came from the jungle
Of the shop to this exposure. Nor do I soothe
My happily married sister who is howling.
The undertaker's men are sad and laugh only
When they think we are not looking.
Now they creak reverently as they plug
This hole in the earth with my father.

And now the coffin goes down under my eyes,
Below my feet and I see the silver plaque
That I know means so much to my stepmother
And suddenly to me. For it bears my name
Which is my father's too. The clergyman
Explains that my father has gone ahead.
I fear he has gone in my stead.
Inside the grave it is already getting dark
And down there the silver plaque twinkles
A medal on the dead.

Telling Them

Every twilight the old weaver came back
To his attic, worked till the sun rose
On medieval dew and hares.
Never having been told he was dying
He did not know he was dead,
And left always in the rhythm of returning.

His son, at first touched, later maddened,
Called for the parish priest, who brought
His bell, his book, his candle to the full house
Where he read and he lit and he rang
To tell the old man the truth, to *tell* him.
The weaver left finally. His son succeeded.

The hand-loom and the trappings
Make it seem like a quite enjoyable story.
But today it is no entertainment
Not to have told your father
That he had terminal cancer.
Night after night he innocently bounds
Into your dreams, confident as a dog
That he exists and is welcome.
You suffer and sweat and cry out. But at last
You suspect that he knew
All along, the old ghost.

Creed of Mr Nicholas Culpeper

Nothing grows in vain. Use plants to heal.
Self-centredly like animals they carry
A thick strong vein of health that can
Be tapped. To have no money
Is frightening, but disease kills fright and all.
Kick men when they come at you with a knife.
Easier to cheat a man out of his life
Than of a groat. Trust herbs. The King's Evil
Does not need a king, only some celandine.

Commonsense and the planets both will help you.
If a herb is of the Sun and under
Leo, wait for them, for they
Must move, not you. And ponder
On the strength of the body that you give it to.
Knee-holly, for example, belongs to Mars
And can be much too gallant for our wars.
Mountain mint defies worms and the ague
But works on female subjects over-violently.

Beware of quacks. They tell you that a carrot
Helps to ease wind – which is certainly true –
But without saying that it can breed
Wind in the first place. Two
Uses of one plant is good. Wear it
As a poultice for the spleen – I speak of broom –
Or turn it upside down to sweep a room.
Colour must be appropriate. The merit
Of scarlet centaury is to reign over blood.

I did not grow in vain myself, for three
Hundred years hence you will still doubt the knife,
And root for remedies like mine.
Plants and eternal life
Have much in common, but remember me
Who show you the significance of time.
Death grew on purpose too, and in my prime
He picked me at full moon one January
And turned me into some concoction of his own.

Return to Sedgemoor

'Battle of Sedgemoor. Come and bring your friends.'
And so they have I see. Dragging me down
Into this pageant of what was once real.
I died here but I cannot now recall
Which side I fought on. And until today –
Comfortable in warm weather hoping something,
Tetchy in winter dreading everything –
I've been content simply to know I was
Once here. How shocking the oblivion
Of coming back to sight and sound, to north
And south, to right and wrong, at a complete loss.

The cows are gazing at the popping cannon.
What roars they must have heard to go on chewing
At noise that shot the meat out of our mouths.
I seem to see the guns for the first time,
Plump little pigs. I hear a voice explaining
That they were known as 'Hot Lips' and 'Sweet Lips'.
I swear we never called them anything
Like that. I first made love on a battlefield,
I remember – though not which or who –
And realized there was a difference
Between love and war: I don't remember what.

Sedgemoor took place at night, and it's enough
To make a ghost laugh in the sun to see
These fluent creatures dash about regardless
While we, with elbows, knees and arse and chin
Stuck out at angles, had to feel our way.
These willow trees were low and strong to hang
Men in the morning light – as they are doing
Now – but in the dark they merely gave
Us bloody noses. Memory does not return
Like experience, more like imagination:
How it would have been if, how it must.

'The last battle to be fought on English soil'
The voice concludes. No riots, no pretenders
Or invaders in what must be years?
No, I am a ghost and do not wish
To understand the present. Let me

Concentrate on getting my life back.
My memory is like a severed muscle
And there's no friend or foe or animal
To recognize me. On the night I died
King's men and rebels all hastened away
As if some moon came up to light them home.

Four Spells

(based on a medieval cure for scalds)

Two angels came from the West.
The one brought desire, the other brought frost.
Out prude! In lust!
In the name of the Father, Son and Holy Ghost.

Two angels came from the North.
The one praised wit, the other praised worth.
In fire! Out earth!
In the name of the Paraclete and the Virgin Birth.

Two angels came from the East.
The one said, 'Gorge', the other said 'Fast'.
Out Lent! In locust!
In the name of water-into-wine and the marriage feast.

Two angels came from the South.
The one sold life, the other sold death.
Out heaven! In breath!
In the name of the devil, Faustus and hell-mouth.

For a Dead Poet

Even a lifelong user of roads
Cannot always join up
One place with another place.
Back at home he remembers
One sun for each field,
One moon for each hill.

Water is the only true street.
The poet goes everywhere
By water. Sometimes he cuts
A town in half and the buildings
Stick him, then by-passes
Another which turns its back

On the river, that brought it
There and brings him there
For the best view. The smoke blows
Inland and away to the square.
Instead of front doors, drainpipes.
Only a gazebo stares.

What is correct for road-users:
One slaughter house, one fish market
Per town, and the cities teeming,
One church for every village.
The poet observes one ghost,
One hunger and one beast for it.

The meadows separately slide.
The whiskers of the next town
Twitch, the next storm sniffs.
He went past on the one tide
Which even when he deplored
He not for one moment doubted.

Mighty Mighty Witches. Salem, Mass

Welcome to Witch City. Hags with cats
Fly on every flat surface, crass
And innocent, on T-shirts, plates.
Mighty mighty witches. Salem, Mass,

Says a car-sticker. Wickedness has gone
Out of town and nothing worse than foibles
Stir the leaves, at dead of night so green.
Women sleep righteously under the gables.

Where is the wickedness of other days?
Somewhere the mighty mighty witches are.
And I am glad to read the words of praise:
Mighty is good, mighty outlives the fire.

For recently I saw them flying in
Over the ocean, beautiful as saints,
Coming to me, not just to everyone.
Yes, witches, and, yes, mighty more than once.

Seven Ages

Where have I got to in the seven-act play?
Where was I ever? No doubt as a baby
I bawled and vomited as the script says.
I wasn't acting and I don't remember.
I wriggle in the anecdotes of aunts.
And when I get to second childishness
And mere oblivion I shan't be conscious
Or hear the anecdotes of my decay.

Three of the parts I never really played:
I couldn't cycle fast enough to school,
I fell in love but never wrote about it,
The career I took up called for little action.
The fifth is more like me; I must be there.
The justice is well-fed, well-heeled, censorious,
Torn between general and particular,
Dodging at dawn the chill of two-sevenths left.

Shakespeare knew the importance of 'as if'.
He knew it was the only way to act
And that to live as if there were a hell
Is very like living as if there weren't.
Anything better than the anxiety dream
Of being on the stage without a part,
Especially in a long play: seven acts
Although the first and last are played in darkness.

The Lie of the Land (1983)

The Emigrant

Sirs, I beg you to re-name this town
Budleigh. I think I have the right.
The truth that made me emigrate
Fifty years ago
Is constant every year like snow.

There is no question of my going back.
Sailing from Devon was the ninth
Life. Down there the coelacanth
And living monsters lie.
In Budleigh I desire to die.

Roger Conant, born in Budleigh, Devon,
Sailed here in 1623
From edge to edge of the one sea.
Died in Budleigh too.
No need for truth. The name will do.

Watercolour

The trees are parsley magnified.
Along the beach the children go
Through sand that might as well be snow.
The drawing-master must have died.

Fifty years ago that bay
Calmly filled the smugglers' caves.
The paintbrush carried off the waves.
Amateur sunshine came to stay.

Picture, picture on the wall.
The woman limps to look outside
Where in grey air the leaves collide
In their profession of the Fall.

The straight limbs of the children twist,
Summer itself is in distress.
The watercolour stopped, to bless
Them, and the watercolourist.

Waterloo

'Oh man, don't make a noise' the officer
Said kindly to the wounded soldier, who
Went quiet from then to death. Nobody knew
What the battle would be called, nor
Did it seem different from the day's before.
A tabby kitten from the nearby town
Lay killed. The mid-June wheat was trodden down
Smelling of itself and gunpowder.

Smoke stood between friend and friend and hid the weather.
Only the flaring of the guns picked out
The battlefield. The evening was victorious.
Sky and a kind of joy came back together,
Almost too late to show a lost and glorious
Summer day, the sun about to set.

Lament of the Duke of Medina Sidonia

I am not equal
To this enterprise.
The Adelentado of Castile
Is a good Christian too.

The King the appointer
Knows me as little
As I know the sea.
His trust destroys me.

Now winter drips off
The great Armada.
El Draque the dragon
Scuds towards Plymouth.

Once out from Corunna
Battle slides forward.
The churches behind me
Are full of women.

My lookout cries
There is land
Lurching out of the waves.
Where is my home?

Smoke flies from the hills
The fires are staring
Bells tumble in the wind
Our enemy sees us.

What summer at sea.
July, my orchards ripe,
And I cannot count
Those ships for rain.

We pass grey harbours
Not built for us.
The barley on the cliffs
Is our foes' food.

The wind is their weapon.
Council upon council,
A hailstorm of grapeshot
Yet they follow us.

Where is my ally?
I am no evergreen
A southerly gale
Shakes me from the tree.

North, north, out of sight.
No laurel wreath, no shroud.
The sea makes more room
Than the earth could.

A Street in Padua

The street must be nearby. This is the square.
They are still selling emerald vegetables
Under scarlet umbrellas, and the bells
Ring from the right distance. Over there
I used to sidestep out of the noon glare.
Still in the Hall of Justice, Donatello's
Wooden horse is looking down his nose.
That street, I cannot find it anywhere:

Narrow, its cobbles always in the shade.
The rooms I had rose up into the sun
A quarter of a century ago
And chimed with noises from the dark arcade.
All that unquiet life so close, but now
At peace I do not know which way to turn.

Farmhouse Time

Four hundred years ago
When this farmhouse was new
The great Queen was the first to go.
Stiffening in her brocade
In London she lay dead.

After that it seemed
Time really began.
The farmer and his sons
Went down man by man
Into the country grave.
Soft and active as a worm
The heir moved up above.

At the top of the lane
Wars went by.
Cromwell's horses broke the hedge.
Rebels from Sedgemoor tried to run,
Hunted towards their houses
By the bloodhounds of the Judge.

Men live much longer now
Than their sheep do.
Yet all the time – once more, once less –
The passing bell seems to be ringing.
At night all our ghosts
Stand in the walls singing.

Each wind pulls straws
From the descendant
Of the first thatch.
The cat, fed indoors nowadays,
Laps like a watch.

The clock on the night storage heating
Ticks like a taxi waiting.

Pigeons

Pigeons perch on the Holy Family
Carved over the west door, on Joseph's head

On Mary's hand, making them smirk like humans
Who are kind to animals. Inside

The church now, we look out: the birds
Fly through the brown and scarlet saints, and crawl

Like sleepy wasps against their sandalled feet,
Lords of the window, devils looking in.

Then from the street a backfire sends them packing
Only the stolid and the deaf stay on.

The saints are left to bow. The pigeons' wings
Clap round the square like faraway applause.

Poems from Prison

We write from prison. We write poetry.
Our most important subject is compassion.
We grieve for orphans, lunatics and clowns,
The blind, the black, victims of nuclear fission.

We often mention Jesus who was sown
In soil as poor as ours and choked with weeds.
His environment made him a vandal.
God help us to do kind and gentle deeds.

Tyrants have put us here. The violence
That ravages the world is what we dread.
England the great has fallen, our heroes too.
Edward VIII and Kennedy are dead.

We used to live in towns and shall again
Yet in this interval we speak of June.
Although the seasons stayed above our roofs
We gather daffs and greet the harvest moon.

Freedom we cannot understand. To us
Cattle and sheep seem free. Far off our houses
Out of their open doors release our children.
Our wives and mothers take the air like roses.

The Conjuror

Arriving early at the cemetery
For 'the one o'clock', we looked around
At the last sparks of other people's grief,
The flowers fading back into the ground.

A card inscribed 'With reverent sympathy
From the Magicians' Club' was propped against
A top hat made of blossoms and a wand
Tied with a black velvet bow. We sensed

The rabbits and the ladies sawn in half
One blink away from being visible
Although the quick deceiving hand was changing
To flyaway dust under a ton of soil.

The funeral that we came for turned the corner.
They had been right to think the world of you,
Who conjured up for us, a hearse approaching,
An interest in life. Bravo. Bravo.

The Prayer of Father Garnet

The end began with death-watching.
How long, he asked, for him to pray.

At the ladder's foot he knelt down.
'Take time' replied the law-givers

Sure of their own sunset that day.
Boards croaked in the high scaffold

And from his prayer he overheard
The crowd's wit. Somewhere a horse galloped.

Hope of reprieve was noise enough
To keep a dead-tired man from sleeping.

'You are come to die and you must die.
Do not deceive yourself' they warned.

A river wind groaned. He saw the shut
Sky through his eyelids. Taking his time.

Midsummer in Town

It is mid-June. In the stair-well
Darkness has papered every wall.
The air is cool. Clothes feel too thin.
The green outside is looking in
Through the opaque leaded pane.
The eclipse of summer comes again.

Beside me stands the black-eyed cat
Whose yellow stare saw winter out.
Now that the leaves have mobbed the light
Her deeper eyes are stripped for night.
In dealings with the longest day
We use the code of January.

The plants upon the window-sill
That looked so solitary and small
On Christmas Eve, now seem to be
Outriders of the approaching tree,
Spies of an enemy in the shade,
Bell-wethers of the flocks they lead.

Beyond the front door, light and heat
Fulfil the stroller in the street.
Beyond the streets midsummer lies:
Open fields, straightforward skies.
No reticence in country glass,
A tree could walk right through the house.

Under this elegant town roof
Midsummer darkness is a spoof,
The magic of a trumped-up storm
That gives an out-of-kilter charm
To the precision of the pit
Waiting beneath the oubliette.

Hans Christian Andersen

He had the time of his life when they cried
'Fire', for in every piece of luggage
He carried a rope.
Rabid dogs he dreaded,
Hunched up on doorsteps
Out of their wild way to the park.
Escaped them and the crowds
That mobbed the military band in the evening.
He had as many terrors as ribs.
One fear needed a saviour
And he wrote 'I am not really dead'
And put it beside his bed,
His bedtime story,
Trusting that the world,
Though it burned
And bit and shoved, would never bury alive.

Solstice

The idea of solstice
Suits those who remember
Childhood in the garden, watching
The sun move, better
Than those who merely know
The sun stands still always.

In the heat of history
Joshua, the tough Israelite,
Made the sun stop for a day:
More light for killing
His enemies. He was a magus.
There has been no day like that.

Constantly before Christmas
The year like a ship lies down
On its side in the gale, pauses,
Shudders and returns upright:
Pleasant weather, the doldrums even,
Inescapable now.

Coriolanus Leaves Home

There is a world elsewhere.
I go from home, from Rome
And its rigid statues.
The wolf steps down, to appear

On strange rocks, howling.
Children I leave behind.
New gods will struggle out
Of the stars, wings flailing.

Unfamiliar markets and morals
Will chatter round me,
Misunderstood gestures
Place me in faraway quarrels.

But Rome casts such a glare
My shadow will stalk, will sulk
More imperiously.
Look at me there.

You will not hear me making
Myself known
But from my shadow
You will see who is speaking.

The Spinsters and the Knitters in the Sun

The Grand Tour paused at Ravenna. Back in England
Rain closed in from the sea and attacked the windows
But the two wealthy young women
Saw mosaic walls whenever they shut their eyes,
Thought of those craftsmen who could never be pitied
Working for God in the sun.

The house they lived in was already childlike
With a pleasant sense of games still to be played
Past youthfulness and prime.
The curved gallery under the roof was bare
And ready for some escapade, some ploy
Fetched out of foreign lands.

A few miles away, from three-quarters of the windows,
Lay the beach scalloped in bays, and the sand shaken
From a picnic basket when at first
They collected shells in the stretches of daylight.
At home in spotlit darkness they sorted and planned
New life for these vessels.

Years later the work was finished. The neighbourhood
Was drawn in, to view the shells stuck to the wall
Within sight of their proper habitat.
It was a beautiful grotto. Pregnant women
Dragged themselves up the stairs to say 'How lovely'
To the unmarried sisters.

Sunshine turned paler every month, and a pale wave
Rippled through the gallery. They ran their mittened
Fingers over the shells and remembered
Not husbands or children dead, that calm evening,
But the blisters, the cramps and the smell of glue
And hot days well spent.

Bereavement

I was too young. I had to watch
My heavy mother lie on her back to scratch.
They never touched ground again, those brittle feet.
I cannot eat what all the others eat.

Foolish mother, rolling to death, how long
Shall the deserted bare an aching tongue
To call for what is drying up inside you
As the afternoon trees begin to shade you?

Soon he will come, the farmer, and haul away
And hide that sheep, who treacherously
Lay down, where I can never find her
Nor go into the slaughter-house behind her.

The sharp May grass sings under my nose
And soon the farmer will hear a new voice
That lost the day wailing about hunger
But towards nightfall turns to anger.

Saint George and the Dragon:
from an Elizabethan Pageant

'Foh, stand off, worm. The hour has come
For you to yield this place.
Your scorching breath is troublesome
That reeks upon my face.
No lion, dog, monkey or crow
Can bar, with any right,
The way that virtue has to go
And I am virtue's knight.'

'Then learn, Sir Knight, this is my earth.
My dam in days of old
Bequeathed it to me at my birth
And it is mine to hold.
I care not for your warlike state.
Your threats to make me go
Are idle toys. Let parrots prate
Of what they do not know.'

'All beast, you have a beastly mind
That cannot be reformed.
Those who make ashes of mankind
Shall be to dust transformed.
How is't you do not see the dark
That presses on the sun?
You had this land to vex and cark
But now your reign is done.'

'Your chiding words, Sir Knight, forsake.
You are too credulous.
In speaking of my deeds you make
A mountain of a mouse.
I do no greater wrong than you.
As far as I can see
You do not come to bring virtùe
You come to murder me.'

'Then dragon, let us not be wroth
That weigh in malice even.
Eternal time shall slay us both
And throw us up to heaven.
If we should combat, what's the gain?
For one would part in sorrow
Today, so let us both remain
And we'll be wise tomorrow.'

Guide to the Lakes

We climb to Mr Marshall's woods,
Or where we think they must have been,
To see the lake the poet saw
One sweet and lovely afternoon
With yellow light upon the fells
From cornfields ripening somewhere else.

His other world has to be glimpsed
In spots, through gaps: a stone
Pushed out, two branches blown apart,
The holes where the eyes rest in bone.
Following the poet up the hill
We see the lake, once and for all.

Soon now the glow-worms will be safe
From children who are going to bed.
At lighting-up time the unique
White foxglove will be visited.
The summer night is coming on
And Mr Marshall's woods have gone,

Cut down a century ago
Perhaps, yet we have found the place
To which the poet in his love
And showmanship directed us,
A bliss for both our solitudes
As seen from Mr Marshall's woods.

The Lie of the Land

Swing low sweet chariot, forced
Down six miles from the airport,
Passengers tanned, worldly wise,
Homing. Through cloud then rain past
The abbey church he fell short
Of its towers, then to the trees

Beyond the town, cutting through
Their high branches like a mad
Flying woodman. Nobody
Crouching under the roar knew
The pilot as local lad,
That in the night he could see

The water-meadows of youth.
Lower than the trees he turned
Executioner, and topped
Cattle then sheep. But from death
He saved his people. Discerned
The lie of the land, and dropped.

Thirteenth Year

Black curve on the gatepost
Insulting the square bull
With older stare.

Bicycle-chain tail at the vet's
Swinging to bruise black.
A saint's face. Hormone pills
For the bald patches.

Deeper every day into the velvet footstool
Bought for the human condition.
At night a new cry
That terrified the Christians.

Pharaoh-eyed in the courtyard
Acquiring trophies,
Mice that are never eaten
Company for the tomb.

These images come from me not from her.
She is unresentful
And enjoys nightfall.

I watch the shadows of the house climbing
Slantwise and high up the back field.
The east chimney puffs out a black ghost.

Wet Day in the Lake District

It started early, light and water together,
Rain drumming to the dawn chorus.
Later, down by the shore, exposed
Tree roots catch their life in mid-air.
  Miles across the valley
  A waterfall, usually
  A test tube, is seen breaking.

All days are wet here. At their best
The lakes are watermade into a map
Of objects: stadium, racecourse, sea-horse,
Even a pair of lungs. Today
  Impromptu meres, whiskery
  In fields, raise half
  A fence for an eyebrow.

Faces everywhere, solitary walkers
Looking up as if the rain were sun.
The land is swollen with fluid but smells
Healthy. A cloud approaches the top
  Of a mountain, surrounds it
  Like a car-wash, then trundles
  Onwards to the dry blue sea.

The Simple Life

They could not sleep for silence,
C.R. and Janet Ashbee
And all the Guild. The Cotswolds
Were bell-ringing and beauty,
An Arts and Crafts romance,
Though under the daisy fields
Lived the bones of violence.

In cloth caps keeping fit
The lads leap. Ashbees smile,
Urbane in cloaks and buskins
Getting up plays, with real
Shepherds in *As You Like It*,
But lying – like the Ruskins
In more ways than one – apart.

Ashbee made her a bright brooch
After their quiet bedding,
A peacock with bashful crown
But tail high for a wedding.
They corrected Cockney speech,
Left the countrymen's alone,
It did not matter so much.

For Arts and Crafts designers
There was no day of rest.
Except for bicycling
Sunday did not exist.
A commune with no owners
Could have no heavenly king
Nor heaven its nine bright shiners.

The church she did not enter
Had staircases of stone
Children, leading up tall
To their parents, gone
To glory in the centre.
She sat on the church wall
With a man who did not want her.

The Simple Life is inside
You, she said, wanting babies.
It is not William Morris
Patterns, nor gleaming hobbies,
Nor that apprentice who died
At twenty, as the cherries
Formed all along the road.

Marry me, said his wife.
Hard soap and flabby candles
And Edward Carpenter's
Aggressive homemade sandals
Vanished. A town roof
And four luminous daughters
Shut out the Simple Life.

The Known Soldier

The warrior of the bronze statue,
Oriental and furious,
Can be named, not only by experts.
He is the one
Who always fought without his helmet.

In no army, he could please himself.
For years he aired his hot head,
Annoying his snobbish armour-bearer
And his foes who felt
He was six inches beneath them.
The birds looked down on his hair.

Uncovered to steel and glory
He must have died relatively young,
Yet he stands among Ming porcelain,
Aubusson carpets and Tompion clocks,
A self-made man.

Kitchen Calendar

The seventh month of the year,
And the kitchen calendar
Turns over to her,

The Lady of Shalott.
One candle in the boat
Snuffed out by storm, one still bright

Stand over the horizontal
Crucifix, the only jewel
She plucked from the castle wall

And threw onto its back.
The rope in her hand is slack.
The river has its way to make.

No more than mirror-old
She sits staving off the cold
In three swathings of white and gold,

Eyes about to close,
Mouth half-open, glossily at ease,
Hair over one breast in the mermaid pose.

She will soon be out of sight.
Before she lay down she wrote
Her name on the prow of the boat

And this action made
A person of the dark wood,
Like all the ships of childhood.

The gossips at Camelot
Will see nothing but a stray boat
Pleasantly named *The Lady of Shalott*.

And at the end of July
Comes the turn in the pathway
Where all the unseen knights rode by.

Dark Waters

We have stayed out too long. The barge
That slid all day through summer meadows
Is trapped in the canal, as shadows
Wipe out the grass along the verge.

Losing its length under thick trees
It slots into the dark and then,
A pleasure boat no more, takes on
The edginess of working days.

The lamp is switched on overhead,
A dragon's glare to which the light
From eyes of animals by night
And years of lanterns has been fed.

Faces live on outside the beam
But curdled into voices. Air
Hails slowly upwards through the water.
I feel the despairing need for home

That terrorized the child I was
At summer picnics in the park,
And still cannot explain how dark
The water and how late it is.

Transvestism in the Novels of Charlotte Brontë

When reading *Villette, Shirley* and *Jane Eyre*,
Though never somehow *The Professor*
Which was all too clear,
I used to overlook
The principal point of each book
As it now seems to me: what the characters wore.

Mr Rochester dressed up as the old crone
That perhaps he should have been,
De Hamal as a nun.
There was no need
For this. Each of them could
Have approached his woman without becoming one.

Not all heroines were as forthright.
Shirley in particular was a cheat.
With rakish hat
She strode like a man
But always down the lane
Where the handsome mill-owner lived celibate.

Lucy, however, knew just what she was doing.
And cast herself as a human being.
Strutting and wooing
In the school play
She put on a man's gilet,
Kept her own skirt, for fear of simplifying.

Their lonely begetter was both sister and brother.
In her dark wood trees do not scan each other
Yet foregather,
Branched or split,
Whichever they are not,
Whichever they are, and rise up together.

Blood will have Blood

Now the Conference stands up to sing
About the blood that dyed the scarlet banners,
Face after flushed face lauding a vampire king.

At church service this morning all the sinners
Were non-political. The leaders came
To Blackpool as sincere long-distance runners

Away, by miles and years, from the blood of the Lamb
That clotted in their youth: a tourists' stain
On arras or flagged floor, touched up by time.

They would not go to church. And yet they join
In words as gory as a hymn, or God
The Son. I look for embarrassment, see none.

It's getting dark. Today the martyr dead
Of church and politics have heard the glee
The blood in the veins sings with the blood outside.

Lost

In town the storm loosened the bones of the cedar tree
Thrashed them out of its roaring green pelt
And they lay clean white on the lawn next morning.

'Worse troubles at sea' my mother used to say
About almost everything. I arrived in Devon
That afternoon, and she was proved right, years after death.

The storm was here too, blowing its own trumpet,
Holding up the white wings of my neighbour's geese
As they fought like angels in the growing darkness.

That night the news, fraying from the Stockland mast,
Stuttered across the valley that the Penlee lifeboat
Was lost with a crew of eight.

('Lost' they still say when talking about the sea
But not 'souls' anymore.) The waves that mislaid them
Were two moors away and three lighthouses,

Yet when the vicar paused in his prayer that Christmas Eve
There was true silence in the church as though
The lost souls had been found for a few minutes
Who had no time for 'Nearer my God to Thee'.

Icicles

Never so long in the history of the house
Perhaps, the icicles this record-breaking winter
Drop lower and lower over the window,
A bead curtain with crows flying beyond it.

Brilliant as a chandelier in the perverse sunshine,
Grooved like windpipes, elephants' trunks, parsnips,
The icicles sway. A wren clings and swings
On one of them, pecking up at the thatch.

Transmigration takes place in colour.
Brown tips on the icicles are Rentokil
Brought down from the roof. Pink footprints
In the home snow are the farmhouse walls.

Thawing, the icicles come to life, differently.
One draws a knee up with stomach pain.
Two cross feet under a single nail.
Some are pulled like teeth out of the eaves.

The window is tailored. Once more the valley
Is the rectangle that only curtains hide.
And the snow drifts away like Noah's Ark
On a green sea. The icicles are extinct.

Southern Railway

A country dawn
Smelling like fresh food
Waiting to be cooked, raw as rain,
Came over the small railway station
As we half-hopped, half-stood
Looking towards London

Two hundred miles
Away. It was years ago.
The train crept up on us nosing
Through the fields, and we posing
As connoisseurs now
Sized up the rails

That shone from Devon
To the city – and still do –
Anticipating the exotic
Mosque at Woking, the sick
Camber at Brooklands, the way
The first electric train

Would slide past
Our rattling windows, full
Of cunning Cockneys (sea salt
High up the river), the halt
At mispronounced Vauxhall
And Waterloo at last.

Committee meetings
And day-trips to what
Is gallery-fresh now take
Me along this line. I see smoke
Puffing out still, but not
Those wonderful sightings.

Near Sherborne
The train passes the edge
Of a meadow so close it seems
It will scoop up the grazing lambs.
They flounce to the far hedge.
The sheep, grown

Out of surprise,
Know the dragon's route
And stay right where they are
Stirring only when a stranger
Pauses by the gate
With a dog's eyes.

Some Sunny Day

A ghost is singing and the song is mostly
Tune, wailed for some anniversary.
The tone is romantic and the robe is priestly.
Some sunny day, a voice promises, we
Shall meet again, a voice which was not ghostly
In wartime forty years ago. Nobody
Now could underwrite a pledge so costly,
Assure two people they will meet again
With enduring earth to walk on, in the sun.

Pure sun, perhaps, as in an aeroplane
When clouds below are the last ocean left
Or above the shadows when the same pure sun
Slopes with the skylight of the apple-loft
Where we stand. Look at the October men
And at the sheep who since Mayday have stuffed
Themselves with grass. Blurred and casual then,
They are in focus now, and the half-hearted
Thistles feed far from where their journey started.

Rain is forecast for this afternoon
Gales for tonight, but now the valley creaks
Like a hot country. The farm buildings shine
Bright as wet pebbles; when the weather breaks
They will look dry. A late flower in the lane
Stares up like a lost button. Now fear shakes
The apple-trees of Eden, and that tune
Desires us to rake up the past, when suns
We could count on led into honeymoons.

Lookalikes

Seen from the train: two men,
Tweed jackets on stone backs,
Who paced – no wind rattling
Their corrugated necks –

Home to a distant farm,
Leaving what they had done:
The crisp body of a horse,
His expensive coat still on.

For the rest of that shaken journey
Everything lying down –
A trough, a pile of planks –
Looked like the dead one,

Even the square backside
Of an uprooted pylon
That stroked with its long throat
The field where it had fallen.

And as the train slowed down
At last a living horse,
Prostrate but flicking up
Tail or a leg by choice,

Seemed to be in the grip
Of a strong inshore breeze:
Seaweed after a storm
And several dry days.

The Lost Woman

My mother went with no more warning
Than a bright voice and a bad pain.
Home from school on a June morning
And where the brook goes under the lane
I saw the back of a shocking white
Ambulance drawing away from the gate.

She never returned and I never saw
Her buried. So a romance began.
The ivy-mother turned into a tree
That still hops away like a rainbow down
The avenue as I approach.
My tendrils are the ones that clutch.

I made a life for her over the years.
Frustrated no more by a dull marriage
She ran a canteen through several wars.
The wit of a cliché-ridden village
She met her match at an extra-mural
Class and the OU summer school.

Many a hero in his time
And every poet has acquired
A lost woman to haunt the home,
To be compensated and desired,
Who will not alter, who will not grow,
A corpse they need never get to know.

She is nearly always benign. Her habit
Is not to stride at dead of night.
Soft and crepuscular in rabbit-
Light she comes out. Hear how they hate
Themselves for losing her as they did.
Her country is bland and she does not chide.

But my lost woman evermore snaps
From somewhere else: 'You did not love me.
I sacrificed too much perhaps,
I showed you the way to rise above me
And you took it. You are the ghost
With the bat-voice, my dear. *I* am not lost.'

New Poems (1988)

From the Coach

Wenceslas is the driver's name. Under woods
That steam all day and past goose farms
Livelier than zoos, he takes to the hills
Where castles congregate in his driving mirror.
In town squares, hanging baskets of marigolds
Spin as wheels and a high wind bowl by.
Swans rise from the river more suddenly
Than a blown newspaper and crackle towards the frontier.

Beneath them, out of sight sooner, a train
Slithers into the next country, whichever
That might be. We are surrounded
By other countries. They could close in.
The guide moves youthfully but with wary eyes.
She describes the morning of her own land:
'This race was an independent people' she says.
'They were not slaving for anybody.'

Every night in the small hours
A station announcer blares about a phantom train.
Every morning is a new turning of the back.
Our coach leaves early while people are going to work.
We shall not see them coming home or hear
How they got on. The castles we clamber over
From time to time are neither theirs nor ours.
We belong to the inside of the coach.

Middle-aged husbands and wives sit together,
Bookends with no books in between.
We used to go to work, once upon a time,
In our own way announced trains, fed geese.
Long ago we fought in a world war.
Now from our capsule we look out on the earth,
Its dwellers gone into the afternoon
Its disused castles swinging around the sun.

Looking Sideways

The corner of the eye lets in lunacy
More accurately than the whole body.
White admits white.

Past the door walks my husband
In profile against the whitewashed wall
His beard gone white and long.
Father Time, father figure.

Butterflies at arm's length
Dance like Swan Lake a theatre floor away
A shirt on the clothes line
Suddenly sits up in bed.

And only this morning
'The sheep are in the garden' I shouted
Glancing sideways out of the attic window.
White was jumping, some way from the green
It should have been standing on.

But it was the plumes of the pampas,
Round and rampant, snipped off from gravity
And lifted by a strong-armed breeze
Into the oblong of the window.

I felt like a tired Biblical character
Who had guarded the woolly ones
That strolled head-down all day
And dreamed that night he saw them
Floating and flying before God.

Dying Abroad

Writing a book on Wessex shovels up
Expatriates who died abroad, some lost
When parents threw them out into the mist,
Some looking for Lord Byron and escape

From righteousness. I came across Tom Hoare,
Son of a banker, sent to Portugal
To be a businessman, showing a frail
Talent for sin, how he could drink and swear

And fornicate. 'The Nastiest Citty' – Lisbon –
'As I ever saw' was where he died
Some years before his father in his proud
And honourable old age expired in London.

William John Bankes jumped bail and lived abroad
Content to die in Venice on a pension
Having sent home to grace his long-lost mansion
The works of art for which his brother paid.

I could have died abroad. And on high heels
In varicose old age trooped round the square
A new colour in my old hat each year.
Friends out from England would have carried tales

When to their own cremation they went home
About my keeping up appearances
And whether to believe my bag of princes,
Too fascist then and too fat now to name.

In gibberish I would – my English shattered –
Have died, perhaps boasting of some invitation
To a cocktail. Happy in a situation
Where for ten minutes every so often nothing mattered.

The sun shines less here. Nobody can deny
Anything. I have not died so far
But trudge to glory in these mediocre
Fields, not Grade A land. Neither am I.

Election Night

'Politicians are a race apart' says a fellow viewer
Far into election night. We have lost our sleep
With these strange people. The winners, like counting horses,
Have got it right and been led off home.

We see the losers, in a junket dawn,
Heading out of yesterday along the M4,
Overtaking frowsy trucks, driving at ninety,
Stopping on the hard shoulder to confer.

We see them again drawn up before their houses.
Flowers which are neighbourless and neglected
Straggle and gasp over synthetic urns.
The affronted cat holds its back legs stiff.

They are unreal, yet they haul their luggage
Out of the boot like anybody else returning.
We are aware of the contents: toothbrushes and pyjamas
Smelling seedily of gum and groin.

The show is over. Through the window in the stairs
We see the magpie, our own returning officer,
Land on the back field among the buttercups
That make a mayoral chain around his chest.

Aftermath

Today they are mowing.
In a week at most
The aftergrass will rise
Violent from the dead.

Today streets start like petals
Out of the domed cathedral
And the Archbishop gives thanks
For a short war won.

Two minutes of silence
Puff out of the guns
But dogs do not bark
As they did near the village school

During the long Armistice
Of youth, with teachers weeping
Every November. He speaks
Of battle's aftermath,

The resurrection word
For him meaning distress
Not a bright born-again
Magic. Common ground

In the afterfields. The cut
Blades gleaned and the new
Shoots smell the same,
Like things after a fire.

The Third Eyelid

Today the black cat has grown a third eyelid,
A white crescent coming in from the corner,
Overlaying the dark pupil. Her eternal stare
Is switched over to time now. Stress or disease
Has made a freak out of the trapeze artist.

And tonight there is an eclipse of the moon,
A black crescent on lightness. The print
And the negative look at each other
Across the valley, two moons, two cats,
Waiting to see which moves first.

It is a hallowe'en out of season.
Informally the souls whirl round the fields,
Tap on the cobbles, scrabble in the thatch.
In the house a radio chatters about death.
The evening air is cool with portents.

Goodbye to the round moon and the perfect eye
And tomorrow. Seventeen years old, the cat
Should be the first to crumble away
But the moon can no longer be counted on.
It may scatter before this poem is done.

A wide cloud with an edge as rough as soil
Rises to cover the eclipse. If the moon
Is spared it will draw a tide of earth
Up over the cat, the white sparkle in the corner
Of her shut eye, and her black lips.

The Footprint

A small patch of sand has lain –
It is never less than whole –
For years now, month in month out
On the grey promenade, blown
Through a gap in the sea wall
By a wind with wrecks in it.

The first bare foot of summer
Stepped there this morning, the print
Heavier than all the shoes
Of winter. Did the swimmer
Shake off the sea as he went
Inland to his sunlit house?

The sea will catch up with him
When summer is gone. The wind
Will bring yellow poppies in
From the sand dune and pin them
On to firs. No one will find
His footprint ever again.

His house will creak as bell-buoys
Ring from the estuary.
Gales will put salt into fresh
Water. There will be a noise
Like doomsday as the sea
Hits him with a storm of fish.

Yacht Approaching the Coast

Winds ago the Gordons' yacht
Approached a coast of lemon sand,
Long hills with rivers sliding out.
It was just as they had planned,
The details sharp as glass, clear cut:

City women who had left home
For a month to walk beside the ocean
And past the new assembly room,
Parasols opening to the sun,
Pugs breathing like a well-bred dream,

The villas in their avenues
Strewn against noise with grey-green leaves
Fallen from eucalyptus trees,
The church with a design of graves
And steady angels in the grass.

Where suddenly the tide-race shivers
They took their pick of the white houses
And near the safest of the rivers
In my home town of all places
Sat down beside the other rovers.

But on goes Turner's sailing boat
Through the scarlet whirlpool (past
The Gordons sitting dressed in white)
Dancing, to join an unquiet coast
That he can see and they could not.

Chloe

Died near a stream she could not drink,
Saw it skipping by and remembered water,
Froze in a warm room, lying in state –
Unready for earth till three human days later –

Zipped up in her pink cushion cover,
The wrong side of the silk, in low relief a cat
Always, though when her ears sink
She will curl up into the future like an ammonite.

No orthodox prayers for dead cats.
We commit her to light perpetual,
Buried under a rainbow, no less,
And then a night when the stars were full.

No southerly gale will blow
Fur against our faces ever again
But no north wind can carry her away
Over France and the Low Countries and Spain.

My Neighbour's Geese

December is the nimble month for my neighbour's geese.
Their field is higher than my window.
All year I look up at them
Fighting on the spot
Eating round their feet.
Winter is their prime and they move.

Through the patchy frost, one foot crackling, one silent
They break out of their frame.
A lightweight I carried back up the hill
His beak rubbing
Against my jaw. My neighbour
Was already ill and could not rejoice.

Geese once cackled in Rome like guardian angels
And stood for something in fairy tales
Far away from Devon. December
Seems to remind them.
Along the lane they go
Straining forward like figureheads on ships.

This December, grey in an ashen afternoon,
They materialised in our courtyard
Ships no longer, more like stray dogs
Anxious and blurred.
I found my neighbour
Who said 'Not mine. The fox got mine.'

They were not doppelgangers or ghosts, nor the fox's
Who eats up the last movement.
They were his. But he was sitting
In a hard chair stock-still
Watching his father's farm stir,
And roll like Jordan into the Dead Sea.

Ninny's Tomb

I'll meet thee, Pyramus, at Ninny's tomb.
Ninny, you may have laughed in the wrong place
But you are not a noisy spirit. Now
You are as airless as your crop of grass.

It is a quiet night. The sea has lost
Its voice, though it lies plump and blooming
Beyond the monumental arch through which
They brought you in to your dead-serious homing.

You are the founding father of wantwits,
Thesaurus silly-billy, noodle, loon.
Not verb or adjective. You cannot do
Or qualify. You are a proper noun.

Pyramus, Thisbe, Moonshine and the Lion
Come here, and so do I and many another
Whom certainly the good Duke will not ask
To roar again. Ninny, our clone, our brother.

I think you clowned your way into your coffin,
Your feet up where your shoulders ought to go,
Or turned on to your face to get a laugh.
Ninny, please do not ask me how I know.

The Dance of Death

The dance of death set out from home
Sixty years ago. The man with the scythe
Was first out of the door.

Between hedges his coat hung lifeless
As he stalked along the lane my mother
Thought she had chosen.

Our Saturday afternoon walk led
Up to the common, past the hill-fort
Where the Dumnonii,

Facing the wrong way, were slaughtered
Beside their heaps of sling-shot, by a foe
They had not expected.

Today looking across from another hill
I see the five of us once more.
Now we are dancing.

A yellow ribbon stretches along the skyline
As though the grey air and the dark earth
Did not quite meet.

Against it the little copse scuttles
On insect legs, and the big wood sticks
To the ground like a slug.

A wind has risen. The reaper's cloak
Writhes and hisses round him. It touches
My mother's right hand

And is all the invitation she needs
To follow him in the dance of dying.
Her bell hat swings.

My father holds her left hand and leans back,
Spine stiff as a toy, not to detain her
But to be tugged.

The two children dance obediently,
To please somebody. They are gawky
And keep turning round.

The dance goes on straight and forever.
The only bright patches on the common
Are dead bracken.

Spring Song

One morning at first light
Sound came to our window:
A double knock like a hard heart,
The iambic beat of Paradise Lost.

I had not slept. I looked out
Through a slit of bright morning.
Wave after wave of bird, one bird,
Was breaking on the pane.

He had spun his enemy
Out of his own body.
His own ghost haunted him.
I recognized that fight.

He must have known that birds
Are not as cold as glass feels
At the end of a March night
Nor have crocodile feathers.

He fought every day. Grass grew.
The field rose in a standing
Ovation, as he advanced
For his last tournament.

I am not the person to ask
If he won summer, or if he fell
Slain by his own lance.
In either case spring ends.

The Scene of the Crime

Today in search of violence
I stand where Carver Doone once stood
Outside the south wall of the church
The only place from which he could
Have taken aim. Where spring had stretched
The graveyard grass he shrank and watched.

There are three windows of clear glass.
He saw her step in from the porch
And bob her white way to the altar
Like someone carrying a torch.
He saw her join the bridegroom, take
Her place, wait for the words to strike.

The pane through which he viewed her then
Faces another, stained with green
And moorland by the hill beyond.
Unclouded in the space between
She was his target and his love.
He raised the gun. She did not move.

The shot made all the crows fly up
As she sank down. The gunman fled.
And I stand where he stood because
I have to live the facts I need.
I must learn something from this spot:
If violence is cold or hot.

Who said that fury lingers on
Where it was felt? The holy stones,
The air, are sending me no message,
Nor is this soil with all its bones.
The tinny chiming of the clock
Tells me that nobody comes back.

Daylight is peeling off the moors.
An avalanche to the deaf, it slips
Down to the stream. Raw evening rusts
My fantasy and skins my lips.
The onset of the dark makes clear
That Carver Doone was never here.

Neither was R.D. Blackmore if
The leaflet in the church is right.
I must go underground to see
If violence is black or white,
Away from here where nothing bad
Occurred, to where it really did.